Development in Supply Chain Management

First Indian Edition 2012

VIVA BOOKS PRIVATE LIMITED

- 4737/23 Ansari Road, Daryaganj, New Delhi 110 002
  E-mail: vivadelhi@vivagroupindia.net, Tel. 42242200
- 76, Service Industries, Shirvane, Sector 1, Nerul, Navi Mumbai 400 706
  E-mail: vivamumbai@vivagroupindia.net, Tel. 27721273, 27721274
- Jamals Fazal Chambers, 26 Greams Road, Chennai 600 006
  E-mail: vivachennai@vivagroupindia.net, Tel. 28290304, 28294241
- B-103, Jindal Towers, 21/1A/3 Darga Road, Kolkata 700 017
  E-mail: vivakolkata@vivagroupindia.net, Tel. 22836381, 22816713
- 7, Sovereign Park Apartments, 56-58, K. R. Road, Basavanagudi, Bengaluru 560 004
  E-mail: vivabangalore@vivagroupindia.net, Tel. 26607409, 26607410
- 101-102 Mughal Marc Apartments, 3-4-637 to 641, Narayanguda, Hyderabad 500 029
  E-mail: vivahyderabad@vivagroupindia.net, Tel. 27564481, 27564482
- Beevi Towers, First Floor, SRM Road, Kaloor, Kochi 682 018, Kerala
  E-mail: vivakochi@vivagroupindia.net, Tel: 0484-2403055, 2403056
- 232, GNB Road, Beside UCO Bank, Silpukhuri, Guwahati 781 003
  E-mail: vivaguwahati@vivagroupindia.net, Tel: 0361-2666386

www.vivagroupindia.com

Published by arrangement with
FinanzBuch Verlag GmbH
Nymphenburger Straβe 86
80636 München

ISBN : 978-81-309-2168-6

Published by Vinod Vasishtha for Viva Books Private Limited, 4737/23, Ansari Road, Daryaganj, New Delhi-110 002.

Printed and bound by Raj Press, R-3, Inderpuri, New Delhi - 110 012.

Contents

Foreword

A mastermind once made a profound statement, »Business management is quite simple: It only requires a well-planned strategy – and excellent people to consistently implement it.«

This principle seems as if it were meant for Supply Chain Management in times which are more volatile, and will remain so longer than we have experienced in the past. The more dynamic the market environment develops, the more sure-footedly and quickly managers and staff must implement the formulated strategies. That is not always possible, and certainly not for everyone. In this respect, the pursuit of Best Practice is also the aspiration to make the best out of managers and employees: Develop Leaders! Those who strive for excellent Supply Chain Management require excellent human resources management and personnel development.

We have been advocating excellence in both areas for over 14 years, and since 2008 in close cooperation with the Supply Chain Management Institute of the European Business School. The link between research, management education, consulting and qualification is not only unique in the sense of a one-of-a-kind value-added chain of knowledge. This link is also very effective for the benefit of science as well as practice. For exactly this reason, we support »Develop Leaders!«, the international competition held by the European Business School.

The insights into the secrets of the success of best practices, which this competition offers, are impressive. However, when taking a closer look, it becomes clear that these are not really secrets but examples of laudable consistency in implementing concepts. This book shall inspire managers to adapt the formulae for success from the best submitted concepts to ensure profitability

than the ability to control it. This is bad. The good news is: management boards, top executives, politicians, and academics are beginning to recognize the true extent of this deficit and investing intensively to make their teams able to network. All executive decision makers?

Not all of them. Actually, only the fastest. Those who apply Best Practice. They are currently in the process of completely reconstructing their management training and qualification programs. And that is a dangerous situation – for those who are missing out on continued development. The turbulent developments of the global network will soon be taking them over, along with some very strong competition who was able to get their teams in shape more quickly.

This guidebook reveals how the best-led companies get their staff fit to manage networks and is for board members and top executives along with, of course, managers from all divisions and hierarchies, consultants, trainers, coaches, and developers in personnel and organization – anyone in fact who has to do with business. The revelations passed on in this book are not just hearsay – the best companies will be putting their ›company secrets‹ on display at the international competition ›Develop Leaders!‹ run by the European Business School. This book sheds a light on the best fitness programs, offering a unique opportunity for anyone trying to make their teams fit as quickly as possible. You will get the chance to take a look behind the scenes at what's going on in the leading companies. From boardroom debate to discussions round the water-cooler, the big and little secrets of success will be revealed.

The world we live in is networked. Consumers enjoy the fruits of this network, and companies produce, source, and sell in global networks. To prevent these networks from taking control of us, we need (enough) helmsmen and women to manage and control them professionally and effectively. These managers do not grow on trees. They want to be, have to be, and will be developed within the company itself:

Develop Leaders!

Prof. Christopher Jahns, Ph.D.
Rector of the European Business School

1 Are your staff fit enough?

»No man has ever achieved anything useful without trying to achieve something extraordinary.«
Marie von Ebner-Eschenbach

Ho ho ho, merry Christmas

Do you remember Christmas 2008? Forget about the ›most peaceful time of the year‹. It has never really been like that anyway, but that year it was particularly bad.

On the first day of the Advent season, GM, Chrysler and Ford sent out the festive announcement that they were practically bankrupt and that German banks would need over 30 billion euro from tax payers; car manufacturers quickly announced a series of reduced working hour jobs – and the telephones rang off the hook in the executive education offices of the Supply Chain Management Institute at the European Business School. Our 350 researchers, trainers, coaches, academics, and academic workers had no more time to spend with their families; no tree-trimming, no visits to Christmas markets, not to mention buying presents. The global financial crisis was born.

And because there was a crisis, all the executive board members, managing directors, and human resource managers wanted to spend as much money as possible before Christmas. Some even arranged training sessions for the 23rd of December. The rather questionable choice of a training date notwithstanding: Should managers in a financial crisis not be trying to save money? Not in this crisis.

The good thing about this crisis was and is that many board members and top executives have finally recognized the nature of the interdependencies in their

- Value-based management: What qualitative (ethical and moral) and quantitative (ROI, ROCE, et cetera) values will ensure the long-term and sustainable existence and success of our company? How can we expand and strengthen these values in the best possible way?
- Optimization of cross-functional efficiency: The individual functions have already been optimized for the most part – the expensive and damaging inefficiencies arise today in the functional interfaces.
- Improvement or at least the professional implementation of global supply network management.

Concerning the last point: If we ask ten divisional managers and heads of department in a company what makes up their company's supply chain, we will get twelve different answers. In the past it was said: You can't manage what you can't measure. Now some board members are wondering: How can we manage what we are obviously not even able to *agree* about? The more important question is: What actual skills are necessary to manage networks professionally? The previously mentioned studies both provide reliable information on exactly this point. They describe what companies need today in order to keep fit for tomorrow. The first of these skills is rather obvious:

- *Future competence: The most reliable anticipation of future developments.* The fact that crises hit us so hard does not necessarily have to do with the harshness of the crises themselves. It is more that the really harsh crises are constantly catching us off guard. But haven't we been able to adapt ourselves successfully to every critical market development thanks to our flexibility? Isn't that the principle of evolution? First the markets and environments change, then we adapt ourselves to the changes.

The principle of adaptation does not work anymore.

The only problem is: Would adaptation have helped Lehman Brothers? No. Lehman and many other banks and companies around the world were nothing more than victims of this strategy. The environment and markets stopped changing linearly a long time ago. They are no longer satisfied with the occasional structural shake-up and show what US researcher and bestselling author Nicholas Taleb *(Fooled by Randomness)* calls ›Black Swans‹: completely ›unpredictable‹ developments. Anyone still gambling on adapting to the unpredictable is backing the wrong horse. Adaptation is out, anticipation is in. It's the secret of every good striker: to be where the ball is going to be in a few seconds. It's a skill, and it can be trained. Assuming, of course, you bring in a second one:

- *The ability to think in terms of supply chains.* Of course, we have our supply chains and we are *acting* within them. We are just not *thinking* in terms of a chain of supply. For example, when a chip factory in Asia is hit by a Tsunami, the buyer of electronic components has an idea of what that could mean for him: delivery bottlenecks, delays, production downtime. That is all well and good, but it is not what I mean by ›thinking‹. The supply chain manager, on the other hand, immediately reels off the five direct and indirect consequences of the (impending) delivery shortfall in terms of money, including second source and contingency plans. This is ›thinking‹ in terms of supply chains.

Only a few supply chain managers have learned this by now – and they regularly antagonize their competition with this special knowledge. As the CPO of a grocery store chain put it: »I am not afraid of the next crisis. I am afraid of the day when one of my competitors can manage the network better than us.« These are the words of a true leader. And that brings us to the next future skill:

- *Leadership: Managers will continue to be in demand. But what the global network really needs is leaders.* Managers mainly manage their own functions. The recent globalization shocks have taught us: The problems in the network do not normally arise in the operational areas, but in their functional interfaces. These interface problems can only be eliminated by managers who understand more than just their own areas, people who can ›manage‹ cross-functionally. This is generally accepted as leadership.

Every manager knows, for example, that hardly any more savings can be achieved on a new product once it has left the drawing board: 70 percent of the expenses have already been determined. Nevertheless, purchasing is put under intense pressure to squeeze as many tiny bread crumbs as possible from the miserable 30 percent left over instead of integrating procurement into the product development process from the beginning which would make savings of at least twice the costs. Why doesn't it happen? Because we lack leaders.

Supply chains need fewer managers and more leaders.

Leaders do not grow on trees. They have to be developed. As the CPO from an international corporation once said: »We should have started five years ago!« Well, why didn't they? Because purchasing was still in the basement.

Purchasing and supply chain management have to leave the basement!

Imagine that the board of directors of a multi-billion dollar corporation all received as their company car a beautiful, red – Mini. Funny, isn't it? About as funny as the fact that the most important managers in a company often sit in the basement.

Up to 80 percent of the parts of a product are being produced externally today. In plain English: purchased. And where are these purchasers who deliver this 80 percent of the product success to the company? Often in the companies' worst offices. Called form-fillers by their colleagues, they are allowed a training course about every two years. The specialists who carry and manage the global networks are slightly above doormen (nothing against doormen) in terms of influence and power in the company hierarchy. Best Practice managers are turning these old power relationships upside down with a vengeance which accounts for the ever increasing number of Chief Procurement Officers with a seat on or direct connection to the management board (see also chapter 2).

Purchasers need to transform into consultants

Of course there are reasons why purchasers in many places are still sitting in the basement and not at the table of decision makers: They do not speak the lingo. A production manager will not allow a buyer into the conference room – even if this person heads up a global network – unless he is able to speak in a language his engineers can understand. But a buyer needs to learn that first, one way or another. Since many buyers either cannot or do not want to learn (anymore), many companies have turned their recruitment upside down: They do not hire purchasers for purchasing anymore. They look for technicians, mechanics and engineers whom they can train in procurement and supply chain management.

Cross-cultural competence

We are living in a networked world. We are living in and on networks – but we cannot (optimally) manage them because managing networks is such a complex business. And because foreign countries are by definition part of global networks. It wouldn't be that bad if it was just foreign countries – foreign people are even worse. ›The Chinese‹, for example, do not honor any contracts – as long as the guanxi isn't right. ›The Russians‹ are not much better: Trust is more important than a contract. And ›the Indians‹ will only take orders from the CEO – frequently heard in many companies. This is, of course, just a bunch of crude prejudices. But it is this type of generalization that leads to minor catastrophes each day in the supply chain, and it is not a result of the supply chain itself but rather of the people in the network not getting along with each other. Instead, Westerners complain about the ›lack of infrastructure in the emerging markets‹. That is just an excuse. Sure: The infrastructure there is often as full of holes as a Swiss cheese. Yet even a holey road can be mastered by a rickshaw – if the supply chain manager knows someone who knows someone who has a rickshaw. This is what cross-cultural competence is about. Recently, a chief negotiator of a fashion corporation showed up at the final negotiations with a Chinese supplier dressed in Blahnik shoes, a Strenesse blouse and Calvin Klein jeans. She does not know to this day why the contracts have still not been signed. Even 2,000 euro designer jeans are a no-go in top level Chinese business circles. This is also a question of cross-cultural competence (see also chapter 5).

Multi-project management

Many projects are being launched because our network management is not up to scratch. Every supply (chain) manager has enough of them. So why does hardly anything change? Because in many teams and off the record the definition of ›project management‹ is: lots of projects, little management. This is shown by the fact that schedules are not being adhered to, synergies are not being used, resources are being wasted, budgets are running off course, many projects are finishing below their targets and the supply chains are still foundering despite all these projects. Even worse: As a matter of fact, many of these projects which are supposed to *reduce* the complexity in supply chains actually inflate them even more. We will not be able to handle our supply chains unless we get a handle on our projects.

Negotiating competence

Purchasers do not negotiate ›tough‹ enough from the point of view of their line managers. Even before the advent of globalization, this was a favourite phrase of most bosses. Now they have to negotiate in foreign countries with foreign people in foreign languages. Recently, our trainers heard about an incredibly trivial negotiating problem at a mid-sized company which, nevertheless, always hinders the optimal management of global networks. The board and the CPO wanted to implement global supply chain management as soon as possible. Visionary concepts and strategies were discussed. What should be sourced centrally and locally? Which category manager should resettle to which continents in which key countries? How many millions were available for the project? At some point in the meeting, one of the divisional purchasers raised his hand tentatively and said: »I think our new global sourcing strategy is fantastic, but what should I do about the fact that 90 percent of my purchasers don't speak English? As far as I know, the Chinese don't speak German.« This is the trivial problem. The complex part is: Even if purchasers negotiate brilliantly, it is yesterday's news. In modern supply chains you have to be able to not only negotiate prices but also innovations and/or strategic partnerships. Those desiring to manage a network have to train their negotiators to not only negotiate the price but also the really important things.

Best-cost competence

Let's consider the case of a manufacturer of electronic goods in Northern Germany. A few months ago, the CEO decided to go along with the trend and increase the single digit amount of global sourcing to 20 percent. His scouts were already deployed and had started negotiations with a variety of suppliers in Asia. Since the CEO was already possessed of unusually good anticipatory faculties, he asked one of our Asian experts for his opinion before signing the contracts. The expert caused a bit of a stir when he first refused even to have a look at the contracts. He then did something totally crazy: He looked for alternative offers in a 50 kilometer circumference of the Northern German headquarters. Surprise! The best supplier was not only located only 25 kilometers away, the bid was also around 10 percent lower than the lowest of the Asian suppliers – this was not even considering the logistic costs and had a similar if not better quality, a higher level of reliability and a greater flexibility of delivery. The CEO was impressed.

Low Cost Country Sourcing is out. Today, Best Cost Country Sourcing is the name of the game.

Of course, all of the skills listed above can be seen as trivial up to a certain extent. The point is to implement theories by practical training. This is what Best Practice companies are doing. Let's look at a few examples.

Best Practice: Titan Industries Ltd.

Do you know what the ring is made of that you are wearing on your finger? It is probably gold (at least in layers). What is considered no big deal in Western Europe, America and Russia in certain income brackets is a status symbol in India. You won't get anywhere unless you glisten with gold, showing as much as possible in the most fashionable design.

Titan Industries Limited, part of the well-known TATA group, is one of the jewelry makers in the midst of this paradoxical hybrid of mass and luxury market. Titan's ambition is as simple as bold: »To be the most desired brand of jewelry for Indian women.« That is pretty ambitious, especially if you consider the competition.

Since gold is the Indian status symbol par excellence and seems to have an inexhaustible demand, as opposed to its limited supply, the competition is cutthroat. Far too many want to make a killing from it: Around 300,000 retailers are bustling in this boom sector, a smothering amount even for the huge Indian market. And to make things worse, market regulation is still in its nascent stage. Even long-established companies have difficulties defending their market position against newcomers, aggressive competitors and margin-eating me-too suppliers in this ›struggle for life and death‹ commercial environment. What strategy do you think Titan used in this market constellation? Which one would you choose? What kind of strategy can a management board choose if they plan to form the most highly desired brand on the market?

Companies cannot be innovative. Only the employees can.

Titan decided many years ago to make tenacious innovation its strategic competitive advantage. Their assumption was that leading in innovation will keep the margins high. Thrilled customers breathless with excitement buy the most, the most often, the most expensive, and the most loyally. The only catch is: A company can not be innovative per se. Neither could you or I invite a company to tea. It won't fit on my or your sofa.

In other words: Companies cannot be innovative. Only the employees and managers of a company can.

Now there's the crux of the matter: How can I make my employees so creative and innovative that the company will become an innovation leader and permanently shake off the competition?

To lay golden eggs

To survive,Titan needs imaginative, ambitious, aspiring, laterally thinking, creative, innovative, resourceful, slightly subversive, and performance-oriented employees who can continually get one over on the competition. But how to find them?

Titans answer is called Innovation Incubation Process – an interesting metaphor: The Indians view their innovation process as an incubator of ideas. That is a glaring contrast to the perception of innovation in most other countries, for example to the German ›drawing-board‹ innovator or the American garage inventors. Titan subdivided the higher-level innovation processes into individual partial processes, for example:

- *Ideas Unlimited:* Employees brainstorm together with their line managers – a pretty uncommon way of creating ideas, even for companies from the West. Normally, the creativity of employees will disappear as soon as the boss enters the room. For the traditionally very hierarchical mindset of Indian corporate culture, Ideas Unlimited is nothing short of a small revolution.

- *SEED:* An acronym for a process which is closest in nature to the classic form of a suggestion system, it generates about 800 suggestions annually. Compared to the normal output of classic suggestion boxes, it is a fairly stately number.
- *What's New?* is the name given to monthly meetings of the heads of departments – nothing out of the ordinary. In this case, however, each department is allowed to say what's new with them and what innovations are being developed. These ideas are put on the ›What's New‹ board to compete with the ideas from other departments.
- *Imagination Breakthrough:* a sub-process with a superb motto, »Challenge the obvious and safe!« A big winner without a doubt: Just try saying that to a German engineer. They live for safety and obviousness. Or an American. They'll counter with their favourite saying: »Don't fix it if it ain't broken!« The Indians do the converse. They look for those parts and processes that function perfectly – and then try to make them better. Their motto is: »The better is the adversary of the good.«

Centipedes won't rely just on one leg.

If you take a closer look at the phases and organization of the Titan Innovation Incubator you will notice the following characteristic: Best Practice is like a centipede. It won't rely just on one leg.

They do not depend on any single tool or process – definitely not when it comes to innovation. They do not just put up a suggestion box – and then forget about it. They introduce a suggestion making process, and a brainstorming process, and, and, and …

Too much of a good thing? If anything, cover as many bases of your project with all the conceivable structures and tools possible, and you will maximize your success probability. It is like trying to find an affordable apartment in New York. You cannot just rely on the advertisements in the *New York Times*. You will have to put up notices, take advantage of your networks, commission a real estate agent, look at notices of foreclosure ...

Such comprehensive understanding can create a lot of possibilities which one-track minded people are normally not capable of. Miracles can happen. I am not kidding.

The three day miracle

Product and process innovations are interdependent.

When amateurs talk about innovation, they usually mean product innovation. Best Practice managers think more comprehensively: Without innovative processes, no innovative products could be produced. And often an innovative process can lead to an innovative new product.

Titan decided, for instance, to shorten its manufacturing process from three weeks to an absurdly ambitious three days. An impossible process innovation? This is another reason why we prefixed this chapter with the Ebner-Eschenbach quote: »No man has ever achieved anything useful without trying to achieve something extraordinary.« Their plan was very extraordinary. At the beginning of the project, neither the management board nor the project manager knew if their goal would be achieved or whether it was even possible to achieve.

The best innovations often emerge in open processes: No one knows what will come of it. One simply gives it a try.

Only a few companies can handle this level of uncertainty. Imagine telling your boss about an idea for a new product (you don't quite know yet what it will do, of course): »What kind of nonsense is that? You don't know if it'll work? And I am supposed to allocate money for it in the budget?«

Titan could handle creative uncertainty. In plain English: They just gave it a try. And look here, after a few weeks, the project team had actually managed to develop a few promising ideas and shorten the process to a degree that has since been called the »Three Day Miracle«.

You do not have to be a process cost analyst or controller to work out what this reduction in process time meant to their costs, their delivery flexibility and their sales power. It is not for nothing that the Titan employees call it a miracle. It is also not difficult to imagine the nasty surprise for the competition: No competitor could possibly counter such a leap of innovation.

The real issue is, however: How can employees become so innovative?

The school of ideas

Employees are never creative enough. But they can be trained.

We all wish our employees to be Nobel prize winner candidates from birth, don't we? Well, I do not know a single Best Practice manager who wishes so. Best Practice managers have an amazing ability to stay realistic. They know: Employees are never creative enough. But their creative capability can be trained.

In India, people have not yet developed the typical Western dislike of all scholastic matters. That is why they named the place at Titan where managers are made strong the Innovation School of Management. You're probably thinking »big deal«: Yet ›normal‹ managers are always complaining that their employees are not innovative enough. Best Practice managers do not complain, they send them to school.

Innovation can be learned.

A good example of this is a ring that is inlaid with jewels. The designers at Titan had thought up a few very beautiful new pieces. There was a problem, however, in the realization: Setting stones by hand in a mass market is an absurdly elaborate exercise. It is like putting a hand-carved dashboard in a VW Bug: impossible. So the stones could not be set by hand, they had to be applied with a load-bearing assembly onto the flat ring, in other words, by stone setters. A quite costly and time-consuming process with a high scrap rate. Even if the stone setters' hands were as calm as a surgeon's: At some point one of the stones will be put in askew. Who cares – as long as the rings can be sold easily and bring in a good profit!

If you cannot innovate a process try innovating what comes before or after.

At Titan they think differently: »Challenge the obvious!« Production management tried everything they could to reduce time and costs in the process. But all attempts to accelerate things failed: The stone setting employees were so motivated they were working with stop watches. If you work eight hours embedding tiny gemstones into little rings with the exactitude of fractions of a millimeter, you are going to be as exhausted at the end of your shift as a decathlete. It was at this point that the tuition fees paid by Titan for its Innovation School of Management paid off: Innovation is transferable to a certain extent. For example, you can learn the principles of innovation. One of them is: If you cannot innovate a process – try innovating what comes before or after.

Because Titan was unable to innovate the ›stone setting‹ work process the way they wanted to, the project team looked at the processes which came before: casting and molding. The caster and molder changed their work processes so that the conventional ›stone-setting‹ process, time consuming and laborious because it is manual, could be completely eliminated, leading to a novel way of setting the stones in the mold itself. And lo and behold the entire ring manufacturing process required 35 percent less working time, productivity increased by 163 percent and the manufacturing process produced considerably less scrap – a huge saving in itself when using such expensive materials as gold and gemstones.

A pleasant side effect of the innovated process: The stone setting ›decathletes‹ are a lot less exhausted after their work now and much more able to perform – which is actually not an aside. At least not at Titan. Because Titan likes to meet the needs of their employees.

Satisfied employees

At Titan, this is a strategic objective. Company management should make a concerted effort to systematically meet the needs of their employees on a regular basis.

Not with wild parties and gifts of money, but with training courses, process improvements, incentives and anything else that would encourage employees to become more innovative. An interesting difference: In the West the idea of ›challenge and develop‹ is king, which is actually (for the West) a real improvement on leading by instruction. Titan goes a bit further: Employees should be enticed to be creative and to bring their ideas into the company to push it forward.

As we have seen, the satisfaction is mutual.

At a glance: Fit for network management

- Skills gap despite billions poured into training: network managers with huge training backlog.
- Many companies are training what they need today. Best Practice trains what will be required tomorrow: future skills.
- Tip: Consult the future skills catalogue and use it as a benchmark for your own fitness program.
- Supply chains need less administration and more leadership.
- Existing capabilities, such as innovative strength, can be trained without any problems, organized, institutionalized and process managed (Titan case study).

2 Onwards and upwards

»So the last will be first, and the first will be last.«
Matthew 19:30

Meet Batman

Do you know Batman? You should. Because you probably have a bat cave hidden somewhere in the depths of your basement.

We meet Thomas G., CPO, on a sunny Tuesday morning in a dark panelled war room of the executive suites on the 43rd floor of a German corporation command tower. The entire management board is gathered and reverently listening to the draft concept of their CPO to rigorously streamline the entire Asian supply network with its spend-percentage of around 60 percent. The CPO (finally) wants to implement a cross-country category management system to replace the old, inefficient and meanwhile proven-to-be-disadvantageous competitively country purchasing. In 27 countries for 320 purchasers within one year! Even the normally assertive production boss is lost for words in respectful awe of the huge project, which with an internal value added of below 50 percent can turn around the company and provide it with a huge edge over the home-team competition.

The Chief Procurement Officer is boldly asking for only eight million euro for the complete conversion of the network including structural and procedural changes, new recruits, IT, new investments, consulting, coaching, training and a new facility – which he wants to (and will) recoup in the first year via increased efficiency and cost reductions. His board member colleagues are so enthusiastic that they approve the expenditure with the wave of a hand even in (or perhaps because of) these difficult times. After the final round of applause, Thomas G. leaves the top level meeting. After he has single-handedly managed to save the company and its global network in one fell swoop, he steps into the executive elevator and rides down into the basement of the tower and enters his office, which is at the end of a short hallway, where his 15 employees carry out their work in circa 100 square meters. Welcome to the Bat Cave.

When our trainers and coaches use this case study in training courses or coaching sessions, the point is made long before the story has been finished. By the time we get to the third sentence every good purchasing manager knows the end. Or as Ulrich Piepel, CPO of RWE, the German electric utility, put it in an interview with the German magazine *Beschaffung Aktuell:* »In nearly all companies purchasing is carried out from the basement.« People unfamiliar with business are stunned – the masters of globalization reside in the basement?

A genuine Chief Network Officer would probably not care at all where his office was located if it was just his *office* that was in the company basement. But normally his entire department is stuck there, too, in more than one respect: They are expected to rule the world's networks. They have the responsibility but not the necessary resources. The figures speak for themselves. Our researchers in the field recently asked a representative amount of top managers to confirm these figures.

The figures are doing the talking

German top managers spend on average 7,200 euro per year per person on training their sales people. There is no denying it, sales people are important. They sell. But no one can explain why only a little more than a tenth of that amount is spent on training for purchasers (880 euro). These ›enormous amounts‹, however, explain the current situation in the global networks: Knowledge is power. Gaps in knowledge leave you powerless when it comes to managing networks.

For experts such as the CEO of Progros, Jochen Oehler, the budgeting activities of a company can often turn their priorities upside down: »If I wanted to achieve through sales the same impact on earnings which is generated by a 2 percent cost reduction which buyers can achieve, then the salesforce would have to raise revenues by 12 percent!« That is especially impossible in the current market situation. However, not only the salespeople are getting better training for their jobs than the purchasers.

The training for production staff is being funded, on average, to the tune of 4,400 euro. Controllers think it is just as amazing – across all sectors, production contributes to barely half of a company's value-added, however, their training budget is roughly five times as big as that of the people who make for the other half?

The rulers of the networks are at the bottom of the training hierarchy, even below researchers and developers who still have budgets twice as high. The height of absurdity is marketing which spends an incredible 5,300 euro on training, even though marketing, in contrast to purchasing, does not save money but spends it.

By now it should be crystal clear how the global networks have fallen into a black hole as far as training goes, despite the billions which are spent on bringing skills up to scratch every year. Those managers and employees who are supposed to manage the global networks see almost nothing of those billions. They are expected to steer supertankers without having either the navigation system nor the hydraulic controls explained to them.

Nothing begets nothing. Anyone wanting helmsmen to steer would do well to teach them to steer in the first place. Afterwards, they will not only be able to steer, they will also be accepted quite differently from the other divisions. And this acceptance is the really important thing. As Josip Tomasevic, Head of Corporate Purchasing at Claas, once put it: »How can we make purchasing more sexy? Talent is sexy. How can we get our helmsmen there?«

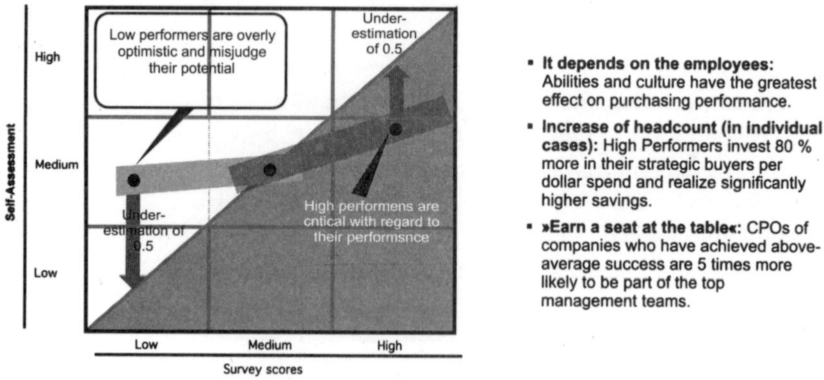

Source: Fortune 500 Study

Figure 2: Results of Fortune 500 Study

The helmsman learns how to steer

The helmspeople of the networks also lack operational qualities, such as the confidence to conduct international negotiations or multi-project management. However, the future needs so-called leadership skills:

- *The big picture:* For decades, purchasing has indeed been about filling in order forms. And now, suddenly, purchasers are supposed to manage global networks? An interesting request. Most of the purchasing managers can count off the price lists of their key suppliers backwards in their sleep. However, they have problems with strategic alliances and category management. Experts are bundling these and other capabilities under the blanket term »strategic networking«, commonly known as ›the big picture‹. It is precisely these capabilities which are required for the management of global networks. Their lack of being far-reaching is an explanation for the sub-optimal state of many networks, to be euphemistic.
- *Acquisition competence:* During training or coaching, when we impart this enviable know-how about selling yourself to purchasing managers, supply (chain) managers or CPOs, we always hear the

same complaint: »I can talk to any supplier in such a way that he reduces the price until it hurts. But it is difficult to talk to our own department managers!« Not because they speak another language, but because the rulers of the networks have never learned to sell their claim to leadership accordingly. This is exactly what Best Practice network managers are currently learning. This explains the slogan of our little competition at the European Business School: »Develop leaders!« We hardly have any leaders – even if every management trainee thinks he is one. We have to develop them first. This means that a leader has to sell himself as a leader even before he becomes one.

- *Risk competence:* How many production delays or product recalls does a company experience because, surprise, surprise!, the Elbe River has frozen over once again, a Chinese supplier has backed out of his contract from one day to the next, the milk is contaminated with melamine or Barbie dolls are full of lead? Since the invention of globalization the global risk factor has evolved from a gentle breeze into a tornado. Unfortunately, the development of risk competence in the control centers of the networks has been nowhere near as dynamic.

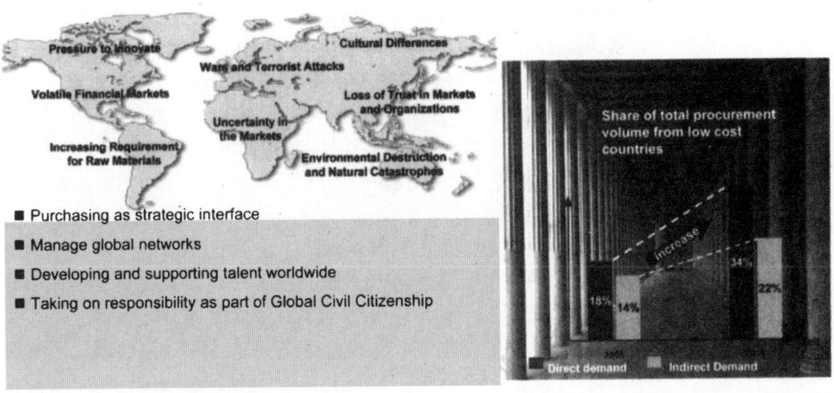

Source: BrainNet Supply Management Consultant GmbH

Figure 3: The management of global development and networked activity concerning risks will become a central leadership task

Recently, some of our trainers were working at a metal processing company which was losing huge amounts of money every month because of the crazy commodity prices. The purchasing manager was almost helpless in the face of the out-of-control price risks: »What can I do if the price of metal is going up and down like a yoyo?« Our experts asked: »Hedging?«

The word was already familiar to the ruler of the networks. But the structure was not right. Up to now the ›finance people‹ had taken care of hedging. This means they hedged everything but commodity prices. People in the basement have no access to hedging, even if commodity prices ruin the company and destroy jobs! This is a somewhat delicate subject: Some companies would actually rather go bankrupt than take the helmsman out of the basement. They are ruined by commodity prices and then blame purchasing for this ruin: »Why weren't you able to buy things cheaper?«

So that it wouldn't get to that stage our team helped the helmsmen, and, since that day, purchasing has been doing its own hedging. It took less than six weeks for the first three supply managers to be trained up in hedging. Interfaces were defined with the hedging experts in the finance department and were integrated into newly developed, mutually acceptable processes. Since then, the wild fluctuations of the commodity markets have not once caused cash flow problems for the company. Added to this, there is a single digit percentage saving in commodity costs because the helmsmen hedge so well. Just imagine what would have happened if the risk managers in the banks (if they existed) had been able to hedge the US mortgage risk? Nothing. Nothing would have happened. No financial crisis, no global economic crisis, no bank collapses, no scrapping premium. Wouldn't it be nice if the masters of the networks could also master the exploding risks of the networks?

If people in global networks overlook ›trivia‹, it is because of the complexity of the network!

- *Complexity competence:* Why are toxic toys threatening our children? Why are so many companies foundering in foreign countries? Is it because the supposed low cost countries actually deliver so little for low costs that the term has now been discredited and replaced by best cost countries or best value countries? Recently, a southern German wholesaler placed his first order with a new Asian supplier. Three weeks after the latest possible delivery date there was still no sign of the delivery whatsoever. The helmspeople of his Asian network simply overlooked the fact that while the local hauler had enough transporting capacity he did not have sufficient refrigerated transporting capacity. »How can they overlook something so trivial?« the irritated CEO asked. The answer is just as trivial:

Anyone purchasing wire reels in Düsseldorf may have to bear in mind three dozen variables – in global networks there can even be thirty dozen. Of course, most of them are extremely trivial, just like the overlooked refrigerated transport capacity. However, juggling thirty dozen of trivialities simultaneously is not a trivial task. It is a very complex one. No one working in global networks today has been trained in managing complexity of this magnitude. That leads us to the last and most important key capability of the network captain:

- *Change competence:* In production, if a machine is breaking down it will be repaired or replaced. This is an operational problem. Networks, however, are a leadership problem. The plain old form-filling purchasing department has to be transformed into network-controlling supply chain management. As Jan-Eike Schuhmacher, Head of the Corporate Purchasing Department at MLP, once said, »An increase in the performance of our purchasing employees is basically not possible without strategic qualification training.« This is not an operational task, but a leadership task. It is a change task that requires change management.

The manager as a change agent

How greatly our economy lacks real leaders is clearly shown in the plasticity of the change itself.

A recent example of this is shown by a company from the food industry. Their management board circulated an internal memo announcing that 20 of its 70 buyers would be sent to a supply chain management training. They immediately received two resignations and six sick notes; eight of the remaining twelve candidates grudgingly sat through the training, grinding their teeth. Were they crazy?

No, they acted quite rationally. Anyone not allowed to attend training sessions accepts the announcement of such forced training with little enthusiasm. Almost everyone concerned said later that the idea alone »to learn something completely new at my age about something of which we have never heard« almost threatened their existence. The people panicked, and the best ones looked for other jobs elsewhere, the weakest became ill, and the remainder closed their minds.

Here's another negative example: The CPO of an electronics company, like almost all professional managers, has realized that he must transform purchasing from being operative to being strategic. His 120 supply managers, for example, should not only be able to negotiate with suppliers, as they have been doing up to now, they should also be able to streamline their supplier portfolio by 50 percent and, likewise, halve their SAP processing steps. The CPO understands change.

He does not let his staff's resistance to change catch him by surprise, instead he assumes that there will be resistance. He knows that his employees, generally, prefer to think operationally rather than strategically and, with a ›shop till you drop‹ mentality, have continued to expand the supplier portfolio and neither manage or try to reduce it. Nor do they follow predefined process steps, with or without SAP. That is why he is using an instrument of change.

He implements a learning check. He wants to be sure that his people understand what he wants from them before they get going and do everything wrong. Therefore he has all 120 employees present their supplier portfolio reforms and the reduction of their processing steps. This goes on for weeks, always two to three presentations a day. After just two weeks of this tour de force he is stunned. At the end of this farce he has seen almost precisely the same presentation 120 times – namely his own.

His employees copied almost everything, word for word, that he had said on the two subjects in his rousing »on to new shores« speech. Although they had understood what he wanted from them, they could not apply it to their own sequence and their own supplier pool. And that is generally inevitable: The necessary change cannot be managed via an internal memo or by means of a lecture. If it were that easy, German lecturers would be champions of change management.

Even successful top executives can benefit considerably from a refresher course in change competence.

If the current crisis was purely a crisis of demand, everyone would be suffering equally. However, this is oddly not the case and we are therefore experiencing a network crisis rather than a demand crisis. The companies that appear to be crisis-proof have the better network managers. What makes them so good is their leadership skills, some of which we just discussed.

Success can be planned: The better the leadership skills, the more successfully the network engines work.

Best Practice companies have recognized this. Let's look at one of them now.

Best Practice: Deutsche Telekom

Deutsche Telekom have reorganized their entire global procurement team in the past two years. »Every level of management has been affected, without exception, including strategic sourcers, category managers, global category leaders,« said Volker Pyrtek, Ph.D., CPO of Deutsche Telekom.

Profound transformation

The scope	Deutsche Telekom Purchasing separated strategic sourcing (focus: increasing value) from operational purchasing (focus: efficiency and quality) within their organization.
The management	Company-wide functional/category-oriented management was introduced. Deutsche Telekom reshuffled internal staff and hired some external staff to fill 40 percent of the strategic sourcer positions and 35 percent of the national heads of procurement positions with new people.
The mission	The mission of Deutsche Telekom Purchasing is to become the number one organization in the telecommunications industry.
The BIG 5	Purchasing is built on five strategic pillars: 1. People are more important than structures. 2. Make savings through IPF. 3. Growth through suppliers and optimization of the value creation chain. 4. Operational excellence. 5. Enthusiastic customers.
The credo	People and their individual performance are the number one priority.

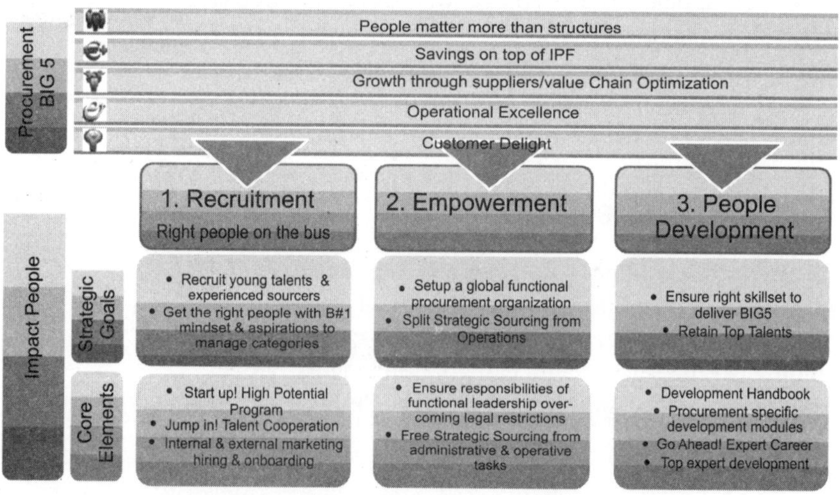

Figure 4: Transform Procurement Set-up (Deutsche Telekom)

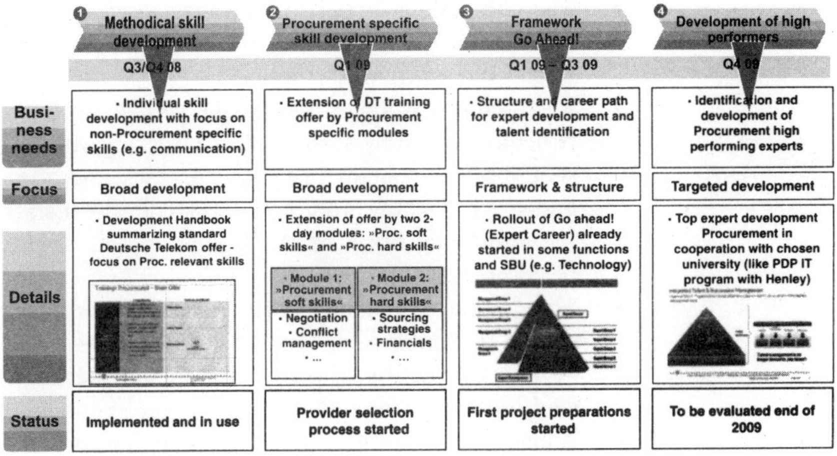

Figure 5: Spezific Development Concept (Deutsche Telekom)

This gives us a nice overview of a very impressive change process at Deutsche Telekom. Now we shall take a more detailed look at the transformation from the bottom to the very top.

Moving on up

The CPO of a mid-sized tool manufacturer with a turnover of some double-digit millions wants to move up. So he embarks on the largest restructuring in his area since the company was founded. He creates an improvement package large enough to make various project managers in supply management weak in the knees. Here is a list of its components which you are welcome to use as a benchmark:

- A third of the positions as strategic sourcers should be newly filled. And by the way: At least this CPO already has strategic buyers whose positions he can staff.
- 20 percent of the positions in local purchasing should be newly filled.
- Some new staff should come from outside the company.
- 80 percent of the responsibilities in supply chain management should be reordered.

- The CPO wants 30 percent more strategic sourcers (via restructuring or new hires) in order to realize strategic cost saving potential.
- Restructuring is important, but the people within the structure even more so; so the CPO, working with HR, should start a training program. (A quick aside: This mid-sized company promotes real HR development!)
- An additional tenth of purchasing volume should be completely outsourced.
- The number of strategic partnerships with suppliers should be doubled.
- As many processes as possible should be standardized, automated and digitized in procurement.
- A customer-oriented culture should be promoted.
- Supplier management should become markedly more relationship-based. Another aside, the CPO will also realize savings up to ten million.
- And since the sheer scope and complexity of this undertaking appear monumental, a specific management team should be set up to pilot the program of change and provide the proper structures and process efficiency.

Within little more than 15 months, the CPO has realized almost all his objectives. The experts in change and supply management are stunned. Why?

Traps and pitfalls

Not all transformations seem to be as successful as the one mentioned above. Why not? Because such a process is fraught with perils and traps. Here are the three most common:

Structures are important. More important are the qualifications of the people working in these structures.

- *Structural Platonism.* Project groups often spend months experimenting with new structures. And this is necessary. But if the groups become fixated on exquisitely designed architecture, there is hardly any time left for capacity, resources, budgets, and, above all, for training and personnel development. This results in elaborately designed new structures with much less elaborately prepared ›old‹ employees. They are still missing the same qualifications as before, so the new structures do not meet the expectations. Often, they yield exactly the same thing as the old structures. The latest structures are not of much use if they are manned by the same old employees. It is not for nothing that the EBS competition is titled »Develop Leaders!«: Structures are important. More important are the qualifications of the people working in these structures.

And here we are not talking of ordinary competences in conducting negotiations or in Business English, but rather of the one qualification which helps people to effectively steer global networks: leadership skills.

- *The Spendthrift Syndrome.* Many companies see price as no object in their restructuring effort. This is well-intentioned. But ask yourself: If the restructuring does not break even and bring in a handsome ROI on top, why go to all the trouble?
- *The Outsourcing Gap.* Outsourcing is still primarily used for short-term cost reduction. Often it cannot fulfill these cost expectations: Outsourcing can do better! For instance, like strategic partnerships, it can free the company and purchasing to such an extent that both may devote more time to strategic thinking, which has to be the real objective of a transformation.

Best Practice managers speak frankly and openly about the mistakes and traps in change processes.

Incidentally, our mid-sized company expresses itself quite openly about these three cases. Its CPO comments: »Naturally, at first we stumbled into a few traps. But you live and learn!« This kind of openness is both typical and extremely rare.

This kind of openness and honesty are the marks of a strong self-confidence. Without the mid-sized company's openness, including the difficult stages of the restructuring process, this chapter would now be at an end. Because what comes next was also anything but easy.

Category management

The CPO of the mid-sized tool manufacturer now wants to finally realize that cost-saving potential which he has been unable to achieve, quite simply because he did not have the right structure; too many operational purchasers, too few supply managers (who also had strategic preoccupations). So he opts for comprehensive restructuring: He wants to introduce category management.

In category management, a purchaser no longer buys everything under the sun, but instead principally, if not exclusively, ›his‹ own category, for example, consulting services. This specialization yields advantages of cost, flexibility and innovation – it also finally yields acceptance by the specialized departments, long sought-after respect and invitations to the decisive meetings. At least, this is what it should be.

The success of category management has in fact led to its inflationary use in practice. More and more companies are making their purchasers category managers. But what initially seemed to be a clever move often turns out to be no more than a change of job title: the same old purchaser with the same old rudimentary knowledge of the category. And the resulting rejection by the corresponding specialized department is also the same only now the purchaser has a cool new title. The advantages of such a way of proceeding: It is fast, simple and very tempting. The disadvantages: It is quickly unmasked and decreases rather than increases acceptance by the specialized departments.

The tool manufacturer's CPO resists the temptation of a mere change in title, and from the start puts the specialized departments on notice that his new category managers will not impress with their cool titles but rather through comprehensive knowledge of their categories. This is why he does not assign anyone to be just anything, but tenders out the new positions internally. He simply wants the best category managers he can possibly get his hands on. This is why he thoroughly tests the candidates in a multi-day assessment center (AC), displaying yet another characteristic of Best Practice:

Ordinarily, a classic AC is performed for the selection of the best candidates for a specific position. The goal is always the same: finding ›top managers‹. This abstract claim implies an odd methodical generalization: What in fact do candidates do at such an AC? They carry out the in-tray exercise, hold group and individual discussions. All well and good – for positions in general management.

The right objectives are of little use if they are pursued by the wrong means.

However, the CPO of the mid-sized company asks himself: »What does the ability to prioritize an in-tray actually have to do with the ability to manage a network?« A university graduate must pass the in-tray test in order to demonstrate that, besides a wealth of beautiful theories, he or she possesses a capacity for structured, prioritized thinking. This, however, is precisely the source of the CPO's irritation: »It ought to be taken for granted that a prospective network pilot is able to think in a structured manner!« If that is not the case, they a) should not be admitted to the AC or b) do not really belong in supply management anyway.

Anyone looking for people with the ability to manage networks should not search for general management abilities. They should search specifically, for example by using a simulation.

Everyone is looking for good network managers. But this search is mostly unspecific.

Simulating and Creating

The AC candidates at the mid-sized tool manufacturer had to carry out simulations for two days. They founded a fictitious service company, set up and structured its procurement from scratch, and defined and implemented strategies. In fact, they did exactly what they were expected in their new positions after the AC. In such a realistic scenario, a trained observer quickly realizes who can analyze, control, organize and manage networks. Not only who has their processes down, but who can architecturally shape and optimize the process structures. Who can identify challenges and hurdles in the network. Who does not merely know how to purchase, but how to manage an integrated purchasing organization. Who does not only understand but can actually implement it. In short: someone who has the makings of being a genuine network manager.

In addition, the simulation also tests the candidates' creativity. After all, it is not every day you establish a company, even a fictitious one: How creatively do the candidates respond to the avalanche of surprises? Do they devise creative solutions to unexpected challenges? This is the main task in global networks. Or as the mid-sized company's CPO puts it: »Global network management is also the art of creative solution.«

The AC also checked whether the candidates had understood the ›basement‹ problem and were able to solve it: How do I conduct purchasing, guaranteeing its high standing from the start with all the specialized departments and with management? It does not make much sense to hold an AC to select the people meant to help purchasing out of the basement if that task is never even talked about!

After this very specific assessment center, the mid-sized company could be certain that the successful candidates had at least understood their future objectives and displayed the best qualifications. This is when the real work began.

The true chore

Those who passed the specific AC with the tool manufacturer underwent training to (further) develop task-specific capabilities. For instance, the capacity to plan and implement a product group stategy. Or the ability to lead purchasing out of the basement: How is a recently designated category manager supposed to present himself to the specialized departments in order to be accepted as a full partner as quickly, unreservedly and comprehensively as possible? For this purpose the tool manufacturer developed the role of a ›provider‹: A purchaser will not be taken as seriously as a provider.

From purchaser to provider, a role change that looks more like a quantum leap. No one thinks of a provider sitting in the basement. Yet, the purchaser must first be able to develop the required ›provider‹ mindset and deploy it in such a way that he can finally deal with his assigned specialized department with the long sought-after equal standing. Almost every company expects this from their purchasers. The tool manufacturer does not only *expect*, but *trains* it.

And as if this transformation of purchasers to services providers was not difficult enough, now the union wants to get into the act.

Unions vs globalization

»When the Germans start a revolution at a railway station, they first make sure they all have their tickets!« A well-worn quote which also applies in network management.

Attention managers! Globalization only functions with a union, too.

Nothing against unions! We need them. And yet when unions all over the country greet the staffing of long-awaited, urgently needed and newly created positions in the management category with a statement that they »do not fit into the pay scale parameters«, laymen and business persons take this in with the same incredulity as when they learned that US banks lent money to people who were unable to repay and without any security. Understanding is a resource in short supply. No one who wears jeans from China or sandals from Bangladesh should take it too far.

The pay-off

In the meantime, the tool manufacturer has firmly established their new helmsmen. An attentive observer recognizes this, for example, from the fact that the new category managers are now represented much earlier, more strongly and more comprehensively in the top decision-making bodies of the specialized departments than the previous ›mere‹ purchasers have ever been. They are being invited, listened to;, they speak as equals among their peers, and are accepted as partners.

And it is precisely this circumstance which displays the demand for purchasing – please! – to be accepted as an equal as mere wishful thinking:

Appeals do not result in acceptance. Competency does.

Appeals are not only wasted effort in this context. They are actually counter-productive. It only takes a few such appeals from a purchasing manager for his purchasing department to be finally taken seriously before no one takes him seriously anymore because these mechanically repeated injunctions go in one ear and out the other. Whoever wants to get purchasing out of the basement should go about it in the way the mid-sized tool manufacturer did: by focussing on category management, a candidate selection that is both painstaking and network-specific, and a training of candidates for their principal future tasks which is no less specific: first, to operate global networks professionally, and secondly, to provide purchasing, as the chief company provider, with a towering level of acceptance, and immediate integration into decision-making processes.

At a glance: Getting out of the basement

- While network management has risen to become the most important function besides production, network managers still have not made their way up the corporate hierarchy.
- On average, 7,200 euro are being spent annually on training sales people. Only 880 euro are being spent on buyers.
- Network managers do not need yet another negotiation skills training, but a training in leadership skills: Develop Leaders!
- Tip: The most important leadership skills are: strategic capabilities, acquisition strengths, risk competence, the ability to reduce complexity and change competence.
- Network managers are transforming themselves from buyers into providers.

3 Star Search!

»It is easy to be the best – if you have the best people.«
Sepp Herberger

What's the most important thing?

Just how dumb is today's youth? Not long ago, a slogan appearing on stickers, buttons and posters caused an uproar: »What do we need nuclear power plants for? Our electricity comes out of the wall socket.«

It is a joke, of course, although it did not start off as one. The slogan comes from a serious survey of hip school kids in branded clothing, spouting foreign lingo. But when it comes to the basic interrelations in the electrical supply chain, most of them just do not get it. Something else which came to light was that a significant percentage of city kids do not even understand man's most important supply chain – the food chain.

Understanding supply chains is the only way to survive in a globalized world.

Many of the children reacted with great surprise when the researchers told them that milk did not come from Mr Safeway, as they had suspected, but from an animal of all things. Fortunately, some of the kids knew the answer: »Cows? You mean these purple animals from the Milka chocolate adverts?«

What our youth demonstrated in the survey was not a knowledge-gap, but a complete lack of the key 21st century survival skill.

Let's not complain too much about today's youth. As a matter of fact, some of the top managers in one of the richest sectors in the world were also lacking this knowledge until recently.

Everybody knows the New York Yankees, the most expensive and most prominent baseball team in the world. Shortly after the turn of the millenium, the Yankees' payroll for players and support staff was over 126 million dollars (by now it is over 200 million). The

Oakland A's, one of the league's poorest teams, paid less than a third of this sum, the poor devils! What chance did they have? How could they survive if millionaire clubs such as the Mets or the Yankees were poaching all the talented players? For decades the world has been pondering this matter. Then Michael Lewis came and brought his pencil with him.

Money does not win championships. Talent does.

On a beer mat, he caluclated that the Oakland A's had, with what had been for years the league's most pathetic budget, by far won the most games. More than the super-expensive Yankees. In fact more than any other wealthy team. In 2003, he wrote a book about his beer mat calculation *(Moneyball)* which triggered the biggest management scandal of US baseball history. The top managers of the wealthy clubs tried (in vain) to ban the book, to trash it and palm it off as delusional. One million copies were sold world-wide, particularly to the managements of real business corporations, as most non-sports managers immediately understood what most sports managers didn't: Money does not win championships. Talent does.

This talent comes from the talent supply chain. Billy Beane, the legendary manager of the Oakland A's who used to be an exceptionally gifted baseball player, understands a lot about baseball. However, the reason why, season after season, he can thumb his nose at the wealthy clubs is that he understands more about his talent supply chain. It is for this reason that non-sports managers find *Moneyball* so fascinating. Just how can it be done – recruiting the best in the industry for practically next to nothing? Hardly a trivial question. These days it is the talent supply chain that determines whether a company shines or fails, as the current crisis is teaching us.

The talent magnet

What do managers complain about most when it comes to the topic of ›good people‹? That it is so difficult to develop them? No. They bemoan the fact that it is so difficult »to get hold of any«.

Searching for talent does not begin with development but with recruitment.

Ulrich Piepel, CPO of the RWE Energy Supplier, puts it more candidly: »Even the best training in the world cannot transform an old nag into a race horse.« So you shouldn't train old nags but recruit race horses from the start. Unfortunately, people are not horses. Even a city child can immediately tell a Lippizan horse from an old nag, but you cannot tell a genuine high potential by the color of his hide.

The industries' best often end up at the same companies.

Why do the best end up at the same companies? Do some managers have talent magnets stashed away in their bags? In a way, yes. They are just better at spotting talent than their less talented colleagues. And there are good reasons for this. To name just three:

- In many companies, the best people among the internal ranks remain undiscovered while others are hired and stuck into management development programs. Managers with magnets focus more closely on ability and potential. They are able to tell the performers from the others.
- In many places prophets are not recognized within their own ranks. Recruitment is often mistaken for external recruitment exclusively. By contrast, the view of managers with magnets is focused on internal recruitment as well. They have established structures as well as processes and put people in charge of screening and identifying (and they are able to identify) high potentials from among the internal ranks.
- If there is any internal recruitment, it often depends on nothing but leadership, teamwork, social and communication skills. Expert know-how, business sense and analytical skills are taken for granted or it is assumed that these have been appraised by the relevant experts at some point or other. Best Practice is different. How?

Best Practice managers will assess, for example, whether a future supply (chain) manager can get on well in a team as well as communicating and purchasing. Above all, managers with magnets look at a candidate's business sense, how acute is it? Does he or she have a clue about supply chain management? How good are his or her analytical skills, for example, in finding out the root cause of bottlenecks and friction in the global network?

Improving recruitment criteria will result in improved recruits.

Or as the CPO of a large service provider put it: »We have the best talent because we have the best recruitment procedure.« What does that mean? How do these magnets work to attract the best?

The manager's magnet

Managers with talent magnets work more specifically than their colleagues, with regard to tasks as well as companies. Most recruiters, for example, test their candidates'analytical skills by using intelligence tests. It is well intentioned but identifies the wrong candidates. If a candidate is the fastest at solving Sudoku puzzles, it does not mean that he will be able to analyze and anticipate the next supply shock. General analytical tests tend to favor the wrong type of candidates. That is why the recruiters of a certain multinational company would present their talent candidates with an empty decision tree for a company-specific problem in the field of organic commodity procurement. Even a child would be able to tell whether for a given delivery problem, within the company's actual supply chain, a candidate is able to consider each and every case logically and thoroughly including all the ramifications.

Talent magnets would test their candidates' abilities based on their future tasks.

This applies as well when it comes to testing important business skills. They will usually be tested by working through plain vanilla case studies: »The market for product X from company Y collapses – what would you do about it?« This is well intentioned but not specific enough. Managers with magnets would have their candidates draft a supply strategy for the company, or for a single division, based on the company's own strategy. It is incredible to watch managers in this test with twenty years of experience leap into checking certain suppliers in terms of quality and conditions of delivery only to find, ten minutes later, that as a first step it might not have been such a bad idea to first assess whether they wanted to hang on to this supplier at all.

At this point, some managers will fly into a rage: »Man, if this is what you're supposed to do, why can't the people in charge get it right when looking for the best people?« By ›people in charge‹ they mean the HR department, of course.

Once again, it is the evil HR managers who are to blame for everything, right? Their recruitment screw-ups mean that the poor departmental managers are saddled with bad recruits ... No reasonable person will buy that. It is not the fault of the HR department. The problem is resource allocation – how much does the company spend on skills training? And how much on recruitment?

In most companies, there is a gross disparity. Lots of money is being spent on training but hardly anything on screening talents. A reallocation of resources and, above all, the focus of management can work miracles in a very short space of time. I always notice when, after a break of several months, I visit a company and I have to ask with amazement: »Where did you get all these new really good people from all of a sudden?« The answer: Better recruitment = better talent.

If you want to attract the best talents like a magnet, the magnet has to be turned on. If it is on, it will automatically deliver the best talents. But will it deliver the best?

Making the best of the good

Isn't it annoying – you hired the best candidates only to find out that they're not ›the best‹ after all? Annoying? It is pretty normal, actually. Josip Tomasevic, Head of Company Purchasing at Claas, says: »Even if we'll select the best candidates, they won't be ›the best‹ yet. It is our job to transform them.«

Supply chain management is still a young discipline. Therefore, the best can only be developed.

Or, as a seasoned head of purchasing once told me: »For a long time, even our best purchaser has not been an excellent supply chain manager – until the day he came back from his training.« It makes you laugh? You think that training is not particularly efficient? As a matter of fact, you are right. Generally speaking. To demonstrate why, let's map out this embarassing situation with the help of an example of the training instrument most frequently used by leading companies – internal training.

This idea goes down particularly well during periods of crisis when budgets are tight. The company does not have to pay for expensive external trainers, who, by the way, do not have much of a clue »about our company« anyway. Instead those who know the business best of all get to be the trainers. Thus, you take experienced experts from among your own ranks and train them to be trainers. Train the trainer. A good idea, without a doubt. So why doesn't it work more often?

- It's not because these people are lacking in expertise but because they have to deal with an enormous lack of acceptance. Just imagine you have been working together with a particular colleague for 20 years, you know all about his strengths and weaknesses – and suddenly he is there at the flip chart, telling you how to do your job?
- Internal trainers are often wizards in their specialist area. However, when it comes to didactics and methodologies they have little experience.
- Internal trainers do not train full-time, but part-time – and this has an influence on their mind-set.

Recently, I bought a cheap pack of 100 tea light candles in a discount store. The first one went out after ten seconds, the second one lasted for a minute, I couldn't even light the third one. Admittedly, a tea light candle is not the same as a seawater desalination plant. There are hardly any other products as boringly stupid as tea light candles. You'd think that any DIY amateur could set up the mass production of functioning tea light candles.

The tea light candle is the perfect metaphor for internal training programs. Theoretically very simple, but in practice, most struggle with bankruptcy, bad luck and breakdowns.

Bad luck and breakdowns

I have seen internal trainings fail for a variety of reasons. The infamous board commitment is among the less exotic. The CEO draws himself up to his full height in front of his troops, figuratively speaking, and sends them into training. In theory, everyone knows that there will be no major change in a company without this commitment from the management board. Nevertheless, only very few CEOs would muster up the necessary commitment. Is it because CEOs are notorious for being unassertive?

No, it is because they assume in good faith that their HR board members and/or CPOs will take care of that. That is generally right. It tends not to work because of personal reasons. Many HR board members and CPOs are just not aware that this is necessary. If there is no commitment or communication from top management, experience shows that internal training programs won't work.

Lack of commitment from top management = lack of commitment from staff

Then we have to deal with democracy. We have it but we do not know what to do with it. Many purchasing managers would complain: »If I made a training for the purchasers at our foreign sites mandatory, it wouldn't work, unfortunately. They report to their country managers, not to me. The country managers report to the board, not to me. And our board member does not see the problem.« This is how internal training programs result in such failures. A case of bad luck? Not in Best Practice.

In Best Practice the powerful board member explains to his country managers that their network managers should attend the training sessions if that is what the purchasing boss at HQ desires. The board member would make this clear either because he has the necessary skills for supply chain management or because his head of purchasing is already a leader and can advise his management board well.

There is a third way – the central purchasing manager would jet off to the country managers and tell it like it is. Management by flying around. As a matter of fact, in Best Practice, this management method is surprisingly widespread and effective (we will give it a closer look in chapter 5). This also shows that you can do it if you are truly committed to recruit and develop only the best, even if you have to jet around the world month after month. And that is not the only secret of success.

Best Practice: Swisscom

Swisscom are generating sales of around 12 billion Swiss francs, an almost inconceivable amount for such a small country. Therefore, it comes as no surprise that its share of the Swiss telecom market is around 60 percent. From a total of 20,000 employees, 150 are working in supply chain management and purchasing and controlling a spend of about 4 billion francs.

Not long ago, the corporate divisions logistics, real estate, quality and purchasing were operating separately from each other. Now, because of an internal merger, they have been amalgamated into a new corporate division – purchasing and logistics. Remarkably, Swisscom then added to this merger every imaginable training offensive, which we will deal with in the remaining chapter. That is remarkable, because others find restructuring alone too much of an effort.

Ideal for post-merger integration: Attending a course makes people grow together.

Can Best Practice handle more? Could be. But maybe it is quite different: Before every large international tournament, national teams would attend a training camp. Trainings integrate and harmonize. However, in addition to team-building, Swisscom had some very specific targets in mind.

Projects with appeal

Before the merger, Swisscom had had a very good and very large operational purchasing. But the flip side of the coin was that very few standardized projects could be carried out, and even fewer special projects. So the purchasing department processed the orders but wanted to be, and should have been, a project partner. Yet another reason why Swisscom decided to double the number of special projects from 20 to 40 with its post merger integration, training offensive and restructuring. An ambitious target, not least because the doubling of such a figure is quite a challenge in our thoroughly optimized times.

Purchasing departments complain about only being charged with filling out orders. But they also frequently turn down special projects.

At a small Italian pump manufacturer's, for example, the network management has been complaining for years that the developers always specify the most expensive parts in their new pump designs. They evade all efforts of the purchasing department to standardize and bundle. Then, one fine spring day, a development team leader would suggest to the purchasing manager that they should set up a joint project group to look at those parts of a newly developed pump which are not relevant to the innovation. The group would be able to select cost-saving standard parts for particular components.

And what would purchasing answer? Would they leap for joy because for the first time ever the untouchable and highly experienced developer is offering early involvement of his own accord? No. The purchasing manager would tell the development team leader that he will join the project, then he would look for two project team members from his own ranks, fail to find any with enough time – and then would have to tell the astounded developer regretfully that the joint project is off because of a lack of capacity. You do not have to be a nasty person to imagine what the developers subsequently said about the purchasing manager: »All that lot in purchasing are good for is filling out order forms.« And that was the polite version.

What did the CPO of an Asian pharma company say when he read this maxim? »The operational departments shouldn't act up like that! We are doing enough projects with them!« That made me curious. I figured out the percentage of spending for projects in his purchasing department with one of his controllers – it was below 10 percent. Why did the CPO think that was ›enough‹? He simply didn't have the figures. For him there was a lack of transparency. His view was no more than a gut feeling.

A realistic self-assessment is more important than professional communication.

Miscalculations like this may emerge if too much attention has been paid to a saying which, ever since the post merger integration, has been doing the rounds in the Swisscom network management:

It is always being implied that purchasing simply has to talk to the operational departments in order to gain acceptance and early involvement and that ›The Perfect Network Leader‹ should be a rhetorical genius like Gorbachev or Obama. I do not want to disparage the contribution of professional communication to success. However, a realistic self-assessment is more important than silver-tongued communication. Or to put it more precisely – a healthy self-assessment forms the basis of all successful communication. Put even more simply – as it is commonly expressed – self-awareness is the first step to improvement.

Based on this self-awareness, Swisscom reworked its network management.

More room for strategy!

Swisscom decreased its operative purchasing and expanded its strategic purchasing. Since the workload remained unchanged, this was only made possible by a significant increase of harmonized, standardized and automated purchasing processes. It goes without saying that in times like these, there was a total stop on recruitment. This created more room for all types of projects, internal partnerships and more cooperation with suppliers. Purchasing's image changed gradually from requisitionists to project specialists.

The transition from operative to strategic purchasing requires an incredible skills training effort.

Precisely for this reason Swisscom founded its own Corporate Procurement University (CPU). Since the focus is more strategic than operative, it is not about what Swisscom networkers need today. It is about what they need to be able to do tomorrow. What should a future supply chain manager be like? Swisscom quickly realized that one manager on his own is not enough. You need five. Swisscom created five role models:

- Data Manager
- Purchasing Agent
- Touchpoint Manager
- Purchasing Manager
- Sourcing Alliance and Business Division Manager

Each of these role models (the contents of which we want to leave aside for the moment) were further subdivided into the following levels: Trainee, Junior, Professional, Senior.

A profile of requirements was written for these segmentations, categorized further into two main questions – which hard skills and which soft skills will these five role models have to master?

		Data Manager				Purchasing Agent				Touchpoint Manager				Purchasing Manager				Sourcing & Alliance & BD Manager			
	Maturity level	Trainee	Junior	Professional	Senior	Trainee	Junior	Professional	Senior	Trainee	Junior	Professional	Senior	Trainee	Junior	Professional	Senior	Trainee	Junior	Professional	Senior
Hard skills	Business and cost-orientation													3	3	4	5	3	3	4	5
	Market & specialised know-how													3	3	4	5	3	3	4	5
	General knowledge													3	3	4	5	3	3	4	5
	Methodical competence (project mgmt)									3	3	4	5	3	3	4	5	3	3	4	5
	Personal work methods	3	3	4	5	3	3	4	5	3	3	4	5	3	3	4	5	3	3	4	5
	IT-knowledge	3	3	4	5	3	3	4	5												
	Operational & process know-how	3	3	4	5	3	3	4	5	3	3	4	5								
	Expert knowledge purchasing	3	3	4	5	3	3	4	5	3	3	4	5								
	Commercial knowledge	3	3	4	5	3	3	4	5	3	3	4	5								
Soft skills	Self reflection & self development	3	3	4	5	3	3	4	5	3	3	4	5	3	3	4	5	3	3	4	5
	Mobilisation of intrinsic energies	3	3	3	4	3	3	3	4	3	3	4	5	3	3	4	5	3	3	4	5
	Communication skills	3	3	3	4	3	3	4	5	3	3	4	5	3	4	5	6	3	4	5	6
	Co-operation & conflict management	3	3	3	4	3	3	4	5	3	4	5	6	3	3	4	5	3	4	5	6
	Operational leadership									3	3	4	5	3	3	4	5	3	3	4	5
	Strategic leadership									3	3	4	5	3	3	4	5	3	4	5	6
	Analytical & conceptual intellectual cap.									3	4	5	6	3	3	4	5	3	4	5	6
	Reliability & accuracy	3	4	5	6	3	4	5	6												

Scale: 1 = not fulfilled, 2 = little fulfillment, 3 = pass, 4 = good, 5 = very good, 6 = excellent
Source: Swisscom

Figure 6: Skill characteristics per role at Swisscom

The hard skills

In the catalogue of hard skills, Swisscom included, among others, the following skill requirements:

- *Business and cost focus* – it makes sense because squeezing suppliers is part of a buyer's job. Unfortunately, the highly praised cost focus is frequently at odds with the business focus. For example, if I put cost pressure on a supplier who is key to innovation, I will gain a cost advantage but possibly lose an innovation advantage (or the supplier will go bust in the next downturn, as is currently happening in the auto industry). Therefore, when in doubt, a network leader should be business and not cost-oriented. He should know the difference between price and total cost of ownership or even better the difference between price and total value of purchase – and use it in his calculations.
- *Methodological skills,* for example project management. It is the same as with Business English. The network manager should be working on projects all the time. Strictly speaking the job of a (strategically active) network manager is 90 percent project work. Unfortunately, most managers have never learned how to manage projects. And it is one of the biggest management myths that you can do it spontaneously.
- *Self-organization.* The better a supply chain manager can organize himself, the better he can organize his supply chain and the way he deals with internal clients.
- *Market knowledge.* Hopefully, that is pretty obvious, at least in the domestic market. As a matter of fact, in times of globalization, while most network managers purchase in foreign country markets, they have very little market knowledge. Where should they get it from? By the way, Best Practice would work with the local branches of independent international institutes or faculties to gain local knowledge.
- *Process knowledge.* We may seem to be getting trivial now, but we're not. Although network man-

agers do nothing other than use processes, the Mintzberg derivative applies to them: »We spend most of our lives with processes. Yet very few know how they function.« And, in particular, how they can be managed, analyzed, optimized, and revised.

Soft skills

In the Swisscom Catalogue you will find: Self-Development, Communication Skills, Cooperation and Conflict Management, Operative and Strategic Leadership, Analytical and Conceptual Skills, and Customer and Service Orientation. I quoted this long list of titles because the Swisscom Catalogue is such a beautiful blueprint for training: with all these points on the training checklist, the soft skills spectrum is complete (and needs only to be supplemented with the appropriate company and situation specific skills requirements).

At the Academy

If you combine the soft skill and hard skill catalogues, you will receive a very comprehensive program. Above all, it is in direct contrast to the normal qualifications profile in purchasing. To bridge this gap, Swisscom created its own academy. Their program was built around the two catalogs. Every employee in purchasing got their own Personal Transition Sheet with their own, individual development path. In effect, they were taking part in an individualized seminar program with all the development requirements identified and agreed to through self-assessment and qualified external evaluation. The learning experience blends e-procurement and presence training, and Academy participants can find seminar catalogues and registration forms on the intranet. The Academy concept combines three main educational facets:

1. in-house training
2. e-learning tools such as e-tutoring
3. supportive measures such as learning circles, networking, personal coaching, et cetera.

Willkommen bei der P&L-Academy!		**22.07.2008**
Gesamtübersicht 2008 (Änderungen vorbehalten)	**e-Tutor**	**Bibliothek der P&L-Academy**

Die Gesamtübersicht zeigt Dir alle Angebote der P&L-Academy auf einen Blick. **Overview in-house seminars**	Das E-Learning Portal von Swisscom. **E-learning tool Swisscom**	In der Bibliothek findest Du sämtliche Teilnehmer-Dokumentationen der Seminar-Lectures sowie Fachliteratur und themenrelevante Artikel. **Study groups, business English, etc.**
Seminare Theoretische & praktische Ausbildungen in der persönlichen Fach- und Sozialkompetenz. Diese Maßnahmen unterstützen unser Ziel eines »best-in-class« P&L	**Vision/Mission** Die P&L-Academy ist unsere interne Ausbildungsstätte. Ziel ist, die Mitarbeitenden bereichsübergreifend auf die Skills der Zukunft vorzubereiten und durch ein Angebot von geeigneten Aus- und Weiterbildungsmaßnahmen die nötigen Voraussetzungen für eine zielgerichtete Entwicklung aller zu schaffen.	**Lernzirkel** • Business English with Gulfrey Conversation only oder doch lieber ein Cambridge Diplom für Business English? Weitere Informationen bei mir. • Networking In einem Lese- und Lernzirkel lesen wir gemeinsam das Buch von Networking-Guru Keith Ferrazzi »geh nie alleine essen!« und zeichnen unter kundiger Anleitung unser existierendes Netzwerk auf. Interessierte bitte melden bei mir.
Academy Lecture Die Academy Lecture vermittelt Wissen – auch mit fachbereichsübergreifendem Fokus **Academy Lecture: multidisciplinary knowledge**	**Teilnahmbestätigung/Bildungspass** Wir stellen keine einzelnen Teilnahmebestätigungen für Seminare und Lectures aus. Du kannst bei mir aber einen Bildungspass beziehen, in welchem Du Deine Teilnahme an Seminaren von den Referenten/Moderatoren oder von mir bestätigen lassen kannst. Der Bildungspass ist für Dein persönliches Controlling und dient Dir als Grundlage für die Entwicklungsgespräche mit den Vorgesetzten. **Confirmation of participation/education card**	**Links** • Top Training Organisation Platform (HR) • Management Development at Swisscom • Lehrstuhl für Logistikmanagement der HSG • Schweizerischer Verband für Materialwirtschaft und Einkauf • Selfdevelopment Guide – ein Impulsgeber zur Weiterentwicklung • Weitere externe Anbieter • **Collection of links: E.g. official Swisscom HR site**

Abbildung 7: Swisscom Purchasing Academy on the Intranet

In addition, the academy established a ›Performance Dialogue‹: Academy participants talk to their line manager about their qualification requirements and the implementation of what they've learned, so these will become a kind of transfer aid and ›trainer in the field‹. Everyone taking part in training at the academy, receives a Transfer Sheet which includes not only self-assessment but also target oriented transfer questions such as: What do I want to be able to do better after the training? In what situations could I apply what I learned at work? Which strengths can I make use of there? What weaknesses get in my way? Quite a lot of basically trivial questions actually.

Best Practice managers not only have the courage to ask trivial questions. They are also able to deal with the uncomfortable answers.

At a glance: The winners have the best talent

- Money won't win championships, talent will.
- If you want to manage your supply chain, you should master your ›talent supply chain‹.
- Tip: Redistribute your budget. Less on development, more on recruitment.
- There definitely are, and will be for years, too few network managers on the market. If you want some, you will have to recruit them and/or develop them yourself.
- Tip: Automate as many processes as possible and in the time you saved you can double the number of projects!

4 Have fun!

Do you know Kermit?

> *»Time is fun if you're having flies.«*
> Kermit the Frog

Employees want to have fun.

Do you know Kermit the frog? Ernie & Bert? The cookie monster? As a matter of fact, every salaried employee should know about *Sesame Street*. Back in the late sixties of the last century, this multi-award winning children's program found the solution to a problem with which, to this day, most managers continue to have a hard time: Managers need more and better leaders in their networks. But their employees do not want to improve. They want to have fun.

In the sixties, US TV companies were in the same situation. Young Americans had an abysmal educational level. They could barely spell, let alone read or write. TV, a new medium, wanted to do something about it. However, all the educationalists said: »Forget it. Anyone who turns on the box wants to have fun, not learn something.« *Sesame Street* solved the fun problem. Anyone who ever watched an episode will know. Most companies have still not managed this.

For some time now, many board members have recognized just how badly their networks need good people at the helm. But that does not mean that the rest of the crew is anywhere close to realizing that. Every week I meet half a dozen trainers who come out of their training sessions and say: »That lot in there, they don't want to learn anything. They just want to have fun.« Yet another reason for the common management to say: »Trainings are a waste of money.« There is no financial crisis, there is a fun crisis.

It's Fun Time!

The world's networks are lacking leaders because leaders are lacking fun. The consequences of this lack of fun are serious.

Since the beginning of globalization, contractual problems in global business have increased tenfold. The signatories of most contracts do not fully and correctly understand the contents, either from a linguistic or a legal point of view. A tragic example of this phenomenon are the buyers from a very reputable German clinic who bought ›modular, non-cemented‹ artificial knee joints for tens of thousands of euro. Subsequently, several dozen patients had to be ›recalled‹ after their knee operations to have their new knee joints replaced. If you know what a strain such an operation puts on the patient you can imagine the severity of this SCM mishap.

As it turned out, while the supply chain managers thought they had bought artificial joints which did not need to be fixed into position with bone cement (›non-cemented‹), in actual fact they had bought joints which were not pre-cemented (the correct translation of ›non-cemented‹). The buyers were simply not able to read the contracts properly. One of the clinic's surgeons, who was extremely angry, put it more emphatically: »They don't understand English!«

Those who make this kind of mistake every day are not narrow-minded, uncooperative or anglophobes. They are simply stuck between a rock and a hard place. Of course, they could involve a translator and their own legal department in every clause of the contract. But anyone dealing with legal departments will know: Production will come to a standstill because even the simplest of questions will take the lawyers days, if not weeks, to answer. No matter what you do – those responsible for contracts in companies have to be trained in contract law. Because meanwhile this has come to the attention of every board member (wrong purchases can be pretty ugly) at the moment the network pilots are being sent on training programs en masse. And what is happening there? Here come the killjoys.

An internationally renowned top lawyer is lecturing about the hot spots of international contract law. He is rubbing the participants' noses in the wrongly purchased knee joints and other goof-ups. Transfer of learning? Close to zero. That is the usual outcome when you talk at someone for hours on end. Why do those responsible for contracts fail to learn anything even from an internationally renowned top lawyer? Because six hours of being talked at will not produce a successful learning outcome!

No fun, no learning.

You'd think that even a top speaker would know that. Back in the days when he was studying and sitting in the lecture theatre he, too, regularly fell asleep 20 minutes after the start of the lecture. Yet, he studied for his exams not in the dry, main lecture theatre but in his student digs. The human brain has no interface to deal with classroom style lecturing. At a lecture the retention rate is below 10 percent – these figures are available to anyone. Learning studies show that people who are merely listening and not practising themselves will retain practically nothing.

»They shouldn't be having fun. They should be learning something.«

Nevertheless, there are companies where those responsible for contracts could out-negotiate any lawyer and can confidently negotiate in English. How do they do it? It is quite simple: »They shouldn't be having fun,« a board member said once. »They should be learning something at the training!« But in this case the reverse would be true.

Only those who offer fun will attract leaders. The question is – what is fun?

Make it attractive, not descriptive

Best Practice found out a long time ago what fun really is. A few quotes:

- »Training has to be as appealing as it is instructive.«
- »It is not the usual trainer wisecracks and showy interludes that make a seminar appealing but actual case studies based on the practical experiences of the participants. There is nothing more exciting for

the participants than learning how to improve their daily work, to make it easier and more successful.«

- »When we work on case studies based on the practical experience of the participants, it is so quiet in the room that you could hear a pin drop. Everyone is working with enthusiasm because they can all see that it is relevant!«
- »Why are we the only ones in our sector to use case studies based on our own practical experience? Because the others don't want to or cannot pay the costs or they don't understand that people are most interested in their own work.«

»If you want to learn how to play tennis you'll have to seize the racket yourself.«

»If you want to learn how to play tennis you'll have to seize the racket yourself.« As banal as this saying may sound, only Best Practice managers implement this principle because it is too hard to build a tennis court in a seminar room. It may take weeks before two to three actual problem cases with overall relevance, experienced by real employees, can be put into a didactical format so that people on a course are able to learn from it. Only Best Practice managers would invest so much time and effort in order to make their leadership development appealing and sufficiently ›fun‹. Only Best Practice managers know those (external) trainers and facilitators who are able to create such ›fun‹ cases in the first place. The others – well, they continue sending their people to plain vanilla folder seminars – and then wonder why there are no leaders emerging from the seminar room.

Many people still do not really understand what it is that their employees enjoy. You can tell by the inclusion of training matter in agreements on targets, and employee appraisals. The intial reaction would often be: »But that means putting people under pressure. You cannot learn anything under pressure!« That is folklore. As a matter of fact, those ›affected‹ have a different opinion. They suffer miserably from pedantic six-hour seminars and then from the fact that not a soul is in the least bit interested in what they have learned. They do not enjoy it at all. However, when they see that their boss, through target agreements and appraisals, is indeed interested in what they learned in the seminar, they are happy to apply this knowledge; here the emphasis is on happy.

Learning from watching practice in action is the most fun.

Some time ago I visited a French electrical engineering company which was desperately trying to get a group of 14 international managers up to speed on networks. The managers were actually enjoying the training. They were picking apart a case study on General Electric. When they got back to their desks on Monday morning the fun came to an abrupt end. One of them told me: »We are not GE. We are us. Why didn't the trainer figure that out before? None of the GE processes and workflows are applicable to our set of circumstances.« He has a point there.

When I flew to France the following year, this group of managers was unrecognizable. The Frenchman told me: »This time we picked apart three case studies from our own areas of management. It was not only the seminar which was fun. We are still having fun, toujours, because we can see that this isn't just another one of those GE case studies which has nothing to do with us. This is our very own work! And now we know how to work significantly better!« That is the greatest fun we can have. Yet it can still be maximized.

The fun paradox

The reason why managers have too few leaders in their networks is because these managers don't really know fun. For example, most managers assume that a presentation to the board has to be grim. A huge mistake – at least when it comes to leadership development.

When half way through the training our participants ›have to‹ give a presentation to their bosses, board members, and European Business School professors, they do not think of this as a duty but as a chance to have some fun. Of course some of them go weak at the knees.

Yet, afterwards, even the most nervous candidates would say: »At last the grey suits upstairs are showing an interest in what we do! A board member, to be precise. That is really something!«

Fun and involvement increase learning transfer.

People want to show what they are made of, what they learned – and ideally to the management board. They are proud of it. It is fun – and that is why they learn and there is a better knowledge transfer. They get annoyed if they get sent over and over to plain vanilla folder training courses and, when it is over, nobody gives two hoots about it. People want to be involved.

Employees and managers like the feeling that what they do is important to the company: It is made clear when the board member is sitting there and having a serious discussion with them (the emphasis is on serious).

If it is that easy, why isn't leadership development fun at all companies? Because there is always a killjoy.

The killjoys

Only those who are fun to be with can attract leaders. Why is it that so far this principle has only been acted on in Best Practice? Because all the others are foiled by the supply chain paradox:

Nearly every buyer of leadership development services expects his service providers to come equipped with a certain amount of fun. However, they then agree on prices which exclude fun from the outset. When a trainer is being paid for just one training day he cannot be expected to prepare company specific case studies, necessary for an appealing seminar, because he is not being paid for one week!

We ourselves don't fully understand our supply chains.

Such fee mishaps are widespread and demonstrate that the talent supply chain is not really understood. The disastrous price fixation in purchasing has left us with toxic barbies, toxic mortgage loans and toxic milk powder. And now it is giving us toxic leadership development.

Best Practice managers do not poison themselves. They do not calculate toxic cost prices but look at the total cost of education. Ultimately, a seminar which is 1,000 euro cheaper per head but brings about no transfer of learning because it lacks fun and company specific case studies will be more expensive than a highly-priced seminar from a total cost point of view.

Low cost trainer sourcing in leadership development is also out. Best value trainer sourcing is in.

Companies on the road to Best Practice have realized that and switched their budget guidelines from purchasing prices to value based calculations. They now wonder: »How can I identify trainers whose training has sufficient appeal?«, something I am frequently asked. The answer to that is easy. If what participants most enjoy is network tasks based on day-to-day practice, then the ideal trainer has to know everything about what makes networks enjoyable. My recommendation is to ask your trainer candidates simple questions about general network problems. For example: »How can I stop my Chinese suppliers from abandoning me, despite my minimal purchasing volumes, every time they find a better customer?« If the trainer starts to stutter, he only knows about Asian networks from hearsay and would bore participants in a seminar with his ignorance. Why should people listen to another person who clearly knows less about the matter then they do? That is no fun.

Another test question which is highly topical: »One of our suppliers is looking shaky. He has been behind schedule for the second time in three weeks. Does that mean the company is close to insolvency? Do I have to activate my second source in order to keep my network stable?« How will most trainers answer a question like this when it comes up in a seminar? »That is a good question. I'd like to throw this back to the other participants. What would you say?« Do you think such a clearly evasive reply is fun for your participants?

Of course, something always comes out of such public opinion polls. Ultimately, everyone has an opinion. However, when it comes to insolvency risks in networks, managers and staff do not want to listen to opinions. They want to get to know the tough criteria of a sophisticated, tried-and-tested early warning insolvency system. For them it is more fun to have a reliable system for identifying actual risks. This is called supply chain risk management. Does the trainer know anything about this?

No one needs seminars. Everyone needs solutions.

This is because solutions are normally fun (that is why the crossword puzzle and sudoku section are more popular than the political news section).

Simply Best Practice

Why is leadership development not fun enough? Because it is so easily forgotten. Recently, during a coffee break at a conference, a board member complained: »I just don't get it! Our people go into negotiations with future suppliers and don't even know if the candidate has enough liquidity to finance our order in the first place! Last week one of our purchasers actually signed a contract with a supplier who had already as good as gone into insolvency proceedings! How on earth can that happen?« What did this board member say to his personnel development?

Right, he said: »Our people have to be better prepared for negotiations. Give them some training, please!« So this is what the trainer did. What happened next? Nothing. Because the trainer worked on the preparation of argumentation, rhetoric and specifications. He barely touched on the early detection of risk. Afterwards, the buyers purchased from just as many insolvency candidates as before. Why? Because their training was not problem-specific. Their current problem was not dealt with, it was only touched upon. The training was useless. And it wasn't any fun because it had nothing to do with actual practice.

Real solutions for real tasks give you improved performance and an enjoyable learning experience.

In this respect, Best Practice can sometimes be a bit radical. The HR director of an Austrian company revealed to me: »We don't ask our trainers for seminar concepts anymore. We simply require them to find solutions for each participant's three most pressing problems. And it has to be in such a way that their bosses can subsequently confirm the success of these solutions.«

If your car won't start you will not tell the auto mechanic: »Take a look at the mechanics.« A car mechanic does not want a vague description of his task. So you'd say: »The car won't start!« He will know where to begin with a statement like that.

In Best Practice, this is clearly put into practice. Take Siemens, for example.

Best Practice: Siemens

»Half of our seminar program is money down the drain – the trouble is, we do not know which half.« Everyone knows that saying. Whenever anyone says it, I automatically think: »Why do we have seminars at all?«

Best Practice does not rely on seminars. It relies on business impact. Of course we still book seminars. However, the funny part is the business impact: participants only deal with those things which have the biggest impact on their business and with topics taken directly from their field of work.

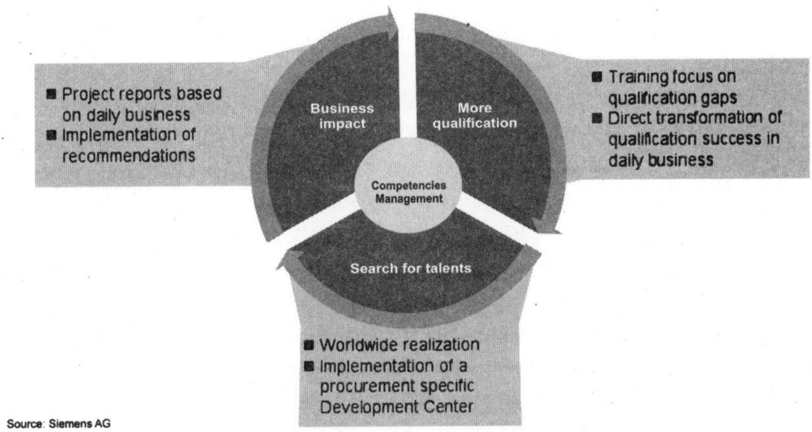

Figure 8: Levers of Siemens Transformer Qualification Program

The Business Unit ›Transformers‹ at Siemens Energy, for example, invited the 106 people in charge of their networks to create a case study out of an actual task taken from their day-to-day work. The strategic buyers among these 106 were supposed to optimize their relevant product group and the operative buyers were to present a model request for an offer in a particular material group.

Siemens Energy: 70,000 employees worldwide and 20 billion euro in sales. Product portfolio: fuel cells, steam turbines, information technology for power plants.

It is obvious that during a training course when people (are allowed to) look at ways in which their daily work can be improved, this is a lot more fun than cramming up on dry, old-fashioned theory because the final outcome results in actual process improvements, cost savings, and increases in efficiency. These in turn enhance the performance of the employee and make him or her more successful and increase job satisfaction. Incidentally, the organization is also optimized. If it is so simple, why isn't everyone doing it? There's a reason for it: A formula 1 Ferrari is more fun than a truck. Unfortunately, not every one can master a Grand Prix racer.

Of course thinking about daily tasks is one of the best instruments for developing leaders. The only hitch is: Nothing comes of it when people do this without ›formula 1‹ type training since they are thinking about their daily tasks on a daily basis anyway – and committing the same inefficiencies on a daily basis.

Best Practice managers equip their employees first with tools for analysis and optimization.

You see, nobody can innately improve their own work. And if I cannot do something, then I do not enjoy it – however appealing it may happen to be! The logical conclusion from this is not that funny: Network pilots are usually not in a position to do their daily tasks better, faster, more efficiently and more effectively.

That is pretty bitter for the world and its networks, but it is also logical: Network pilots were never trained in self-improvement or even in organizational development. That is precisely why Siemens first sent their 106 candidates on a week's training course to learn about the skills and virtues required to optimize their tasks. This investment paid off: Employees were creative to an incredible degree and above and beyond all expectations.

Back to the drawing board

When managers and staff enjoy what they are doing, they have started to change.

If employees have been equipped with the skills required to optimize their own work, the outcome is normally awe-inspiring. So it was for a supply chain manager who presented a new concept for purchasing transportation services which she had developed herself. Of course, the Siemens clan had been purchasing

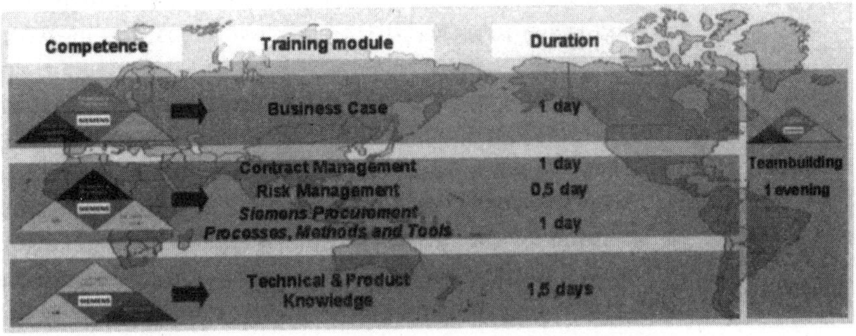

Source: Siemens AG

Figure 9: Exemplary training week of Siemens Transformer program »On the way to world-class Procurement«

transport services all along. Yet what the Siemens lady presented was so new, and so brilliant – as something can only be if someone is completely motivated and it is something from which he/she can benefit directly – what happened at Siemens was no longer training in the usual sense, but rather several small and some larger change projects.

Most seminars are thus money down the drain because they will never be able to offer the same potential for change as a focused engagement with your own field of activity. The same applies to its diagnostic potential: A sample of the work in the optimization of your own tasks is the perfect way to help you identify the best network pilots in your own ranks (with accompanying appraisals). This is why Siemens invited the best 15 of its 106 network pilots to a supply development center. Even this small step is already a giant leap from Normal Practice.

Normally, the line manager will recommend those who should be developed. That is customary, but it isn't enough. A line manager leads. He cannot judge the development potential of his employees nearly half as well as the success of a work sample when it is judged by a neutral juror. In the case of Siemens, the jury panel was made up of the Vice President of Supply Chain Management, Thomas Holzner, and professors from the

European Business School. That way it could be guaranteed that the selected 15 really were the best 15. What happened to them?

These 15 were trained to become what globalization currently needs – network leaders. During an intensive week of training, they were equipped with the necessary leadership skills: methodical, social, analytical, and instrumental. The emphasis was on leadership and strategic skills. They were able to put these into practice immediately after the training. They organized so-called future workshops on a worldwide basis, where all the topics were discussed which would hit network management over the next few years. Then projects were set up for these central issues and carried out by virtual teams. Extra work? Not necessarily.

Best Practice training lasts much longer.

That is why Siemens started the future conferences and continued to let the participants work on their various projects afterwards. Training programs will not be effective unless their participants have to actively work on the issues that were part of the program.

Leadership skills in networks

Specificity is fun and will lead to success.

Throughout this chapter we have basically been talking about nothing other than: The more task-specific, process-specific, position-specific training is, the more enjoyable the learning and the more intensive the performance improvement will be afterwards. This makes sense: If I want to learn to play tennis I do not go out and ride a bike. I cannot learn to play tennis by riding a bike and that is why I do not enjoy it particulary.

What makes sense in sports is almost completely unknown when it comes to the business development of network leaders. Many will say that their people have been trained specifically. Most motorists will say that they are very good drivers (which is mathematically impossible from a statistical point of view – but that does not stop anyone from saying it). However, this particular claim can be easily refuted when it comes to those things which should characterize a leader: leadership skills.

A leader is expected to lead. Yet, as is evidenced by your average dad who seems unable to control his teenage kids, it is the one skill you are not born with. It has to be learned. How? Naturally, in ›leadership skills‹ modules within management development. Maslow, ›challenge and encourage‹, ›leading by objectives‹ – we all know the usual contents would-be leaders are taught about. They are absolutely necessary and useful, but unfortunately that is only half the battle, as these days it is far too unspecific.

In these times of globalization, there are mostly virtual employees.

For most of the day, network pilots will have to deal with virtual teams. The category manager for metals is based in Asia, the one for software in India, the purchasing manager in Düsseldorf. Ergo: With (upcoming) leaders you shouldn't just be training general leadership skills but exactly the specific skills required for the job.

Once again something which sounds very obvious but usually does not work in practice because those who are in charge cannot see any difference between traditional and virtual teams: »A team's a team, isn't it?« Well no, actually. In a traditional team everyone knows each other personally and the occasional contact in the aisle, in the canteen, or in the kitchen oils the wheels of a successful team. Virtual teams lack this personal contact, relationship quality, and informal communication. The consequences are negative.

Virtual teams

Many virtual teams argue more than they work.

Up till now, the management of virtual teams has been rather inefficient due to a lack of knowledge and experience. Even the simplest of processes comes to a standstill because the Brits are boycotting »those impudent Germans« and the Americans are complaining about the »pushy« Italians.

And it is not just due to crude cultural differences. Above all, it is due to an incorrect use of media.

We are living in the IT age. Yet many people have problems with the telephone.

I do not mean problems with modern telephone equipment. Even Nobel prize winners have this kind of problems. These are the so-called built-in nuisances (BiN). It is true, lots of people just don't know when to use a telephone and what to say, or when to write an email or have a conference call.

Recently a German local buyer emailed the following to his British category manager: »Advise urgently to check out steel delivery from China!« Subsequently, the Brit broke off contact with him and nearly brought production to a standstill, because some days after the Chinese supplier broke down indeed. That is what the blundering colleague had wanted to point out – without success.

Firstly, he had adopted the wrong tone. When talking to an Englishman, one should never use the words ›advise‹ and ›urgently‹ together. The British are a fine, reserved people, and well known for their classic understatement. They would have written, and therefore expect the same from the German: »I would like to suggest that you check out our Chinese steel source.« In the German's version any educated Englishman would have naturally assumed that his colleague was being bossy, which was clearly documented by the Brit's reaction: »Who the hell does the bloody Kraut think he is? God Almighty? Elton John? Our CEO?«

Yet the linguistic error could have been forgiven – if it had happened on the phone. The Englishman would have been able to tell by the intonation and the mood of the conversation that his colleague was not having illusions of grandeur but simply being over-zealous as usual. However, there was no way to detect that because the colleague had no idea how to behave in a virtual team (it is not his fault, he had never been trained). To this day he does not know which messages should be transmitted by which medium. He is not the only one.

The entire virtual team is totally inefficient. »The Spanish, for example,« says a team leader, »are sending emails every day which are several pages long but could be summarized in two sentences if they ever thought of picking up the phone. Are there no telephones in Spain?«

That is another reason why his team is missing every other milestone by at least three weeks.

Everyone knows that by now. Nevertheless, to date it is mainly only Best Practice which offers virtual leadership skills training. If I know what makes Tiger Woods so good it does not necessarily mean that I can become just as good. Only training like a champion can make you a champion.

Virtual leadership skills are the missing link in the training of network leaders.

At a glance: Fun is a serious thing

- An internal obstacle to Leadership Development are ineffective development measures. They are too descriptive, too theoretical, have too many cases from other companies, and the transfer distance is too far. In short – not fun enough.
- Tip: If you want leaders, you need more than instructive training, you need appealing training programs.
- Tip: Participants love projects taken from their own field of work.
- Putting together appropriate real life projects takes a lot of time and requires specially qualified trainers.

5 We can conquer the world!

»The goldfish thinks, of course, there's a God.
Who else would change the water in the bowl every week?«
Richard Harris in *Juggernaut*

The Babel syndrome

Germany is a wealthy country. You can tell from the garbage trucks. This became clear when an Asian exchange student wrote a letter to his mother back home: »Mom, you won't believe how wealthy Germany is. They use a Daimler to collect the garbage!« It won't help explaining to the boy that in Germany, although a Daimler is indeed a luxury passenger car, a Daimler truck is just an ordinary truck.

This anecdote is less funny, however, if we replace the Asian exchange student with a German board member, a French CPO and an Italian category manager. While they also tend not to understand the foreign countries they're dealing with, in contrast to the exchange student, this gap in understanding can have painful consequences for supplier relations. A small selection of (anonymous) statements by foreign business partners from our international complaints and suggestions box:

- »You haven't got a clue about our country, but you think it is not going to effect our business relationship? If that isn't naïve ...«
- »A German company buys goods to the tune of two million dollars from us every year. Their buyer's English is worse than that of our little daughter. But if order processing misunderstandings arise, of course, it is never his fault but ours, the out-of-touch Brazilians.«

- »We are the primary source for a French gear box manufacturer. Do you think that their category manager would deign to spend a mere three days a year here? Who does he think he is, the Sun King ruling the world from Versailles?«

Cultural ignorance is embarrassing and an extremely expensive cost factor.

Best Practice would target the Babel factor and start to work on it faster than others. The CPO of a Belgian manufacturer of consumer goods: »Purchasing in Asia is an art. To prevent anyone from trying to pull the wool over the eyes of our local experts in purchasing, development and quality management, our people have to be very familiar with the culture there and, most of all, have language skills.« And that means more than just the international language of English – it means getting to know the language(s) of the country. In India, for example, apart from Hindi and English, there are 21 other recognized languages.

If you want to do business with the world you have to understand it.

And that does not mean just the cultural peculiarities. You have to get to know the submarkets – if you can master those, you'll be the master of the world.

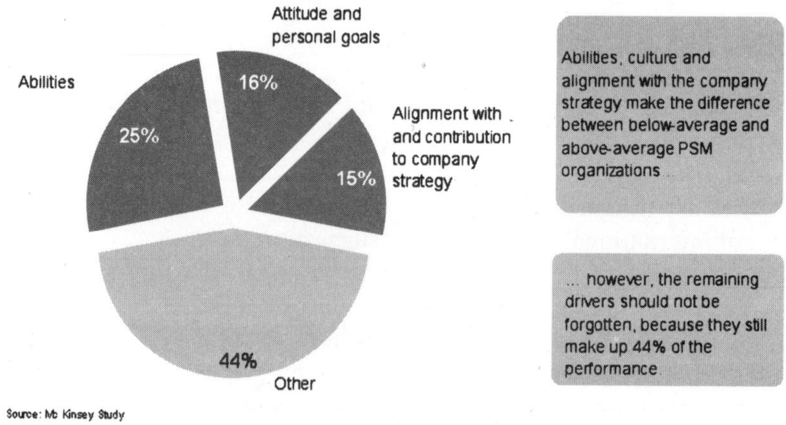

Figure 10: Abilities and culture have the greatest effect on purchasing success

Who's in charge of the world?

Why do so many foreign corporate escapades fail? Why are so many Asian supply chains shaky?

The most common answer is: »In foreign countries we have to contend with bloody corruption, regulations, bureaucracy, and a weak infrastructure.« And that is no doubt correct. Emerging countries are partially defined by these drawbacks. But it does not explain why the failure rates of foreign, outsourcing, and offshoring Best Practice projects or Best Practice supply chains and joint ventures are much lower and rarely encounter difficulties. Although they have to deal with the same corruption, regulations, bureaucracy, and infrastructure! Is Best Practice subject to different laws? Do they have better connections? Hardly. The reason is:

If you have difficulties in foreign markets, you are a victim of your lack of understanding of local submarkets.

Submarkets include, for example, the labor and real estate markets, the banking and the service sector. Dr Markus Weidmann, Moscow Head of SMI Russia, can rattle off scores of disaster stories. Picture this little beauty. It is a lovely Monday morning in Moscow, and the entire office of a Western company suddenly find themselves, and all their office furniture, sitting out on the street in front of their own office building. The locks in the building have been changed the night before.

While the Swiss born Moscow office manager got himself worked up about his landlord's blatant breach of contract, his Russian driver shrugged his shoulders and said: »Russians do not believe in contracts. For us, trust on both sides is more important. Why didn't you build trust with your landlord? You Westerners, you think you're all so smart.«

In Moscow it is nearly impossible to find new office space at short notice. It took them more than three weeks. During this period, the Moscow office was basically ›out to lunch‹ and, as a result, this Western company lost three orders, experienced a massive slump in sales and had to fire employees in the West. And all that because the Moscow office manager didn't know enough about the ins and outs of the Russian real estate market. (Does he now?)

Globalization is one of the biggest studies out in the field in human history. The great experimenter in the sky has allocated a number of managers to foreign markets. The conditions are the same for everyone, including the real estate market conditions. Nevertheless, a few days after the start of the study the test market splits into two groups – the successful and the failures. The first group understands the rules of the foreign submarkets, the second group does not. Darwin would have been ecstatic – globalization is the biggest survival-of-the-fittest experiment ever.

Survival of the fittest

Who will be the winners in globalization? Whose supply chains will be able to run the race? Not the one with the biggest budget and the best product. But the one who knows most about the local submarkets. Pure Darwinian economics – survival of the fittest. What Darwin *cannot* explain is *why* are the fittest so fit? Anyone renting office space in Moscow comes up against the same market. Why don't they all see that trust trumps having a contract (before contracts are ignored)? This has to do with the famous ›management mindset‹.

What is the Best Practice mindset? It does not say: »Today we'll do a roll-out in Ukraine and tomorrow we'll do Bulgaria!« With this type of imperialistic business mindset it is clear that you're going to treat your Moscow landlord the same as any other supplier (»What do the Russians know anyway? Their heads are full of nothing but socialism!«). Best Practice is not imperialistic, their mindset is similar to going on an expedition. Before going to a foreign country it is Best Practice to buy a travel guide and to study the foreign customs and habits.

That is why it is *not* Best Practice to send off newcomers and say: »They'll settle in eventually!« Until they do, they'll have put their foot in it so many times that the subsequent costs would have paid for ten thousand travel guides.

Nor does Best Practice believe in the typically German engineering and book-keeping mentality: »Technology and finance are everything!« In the age of globalization they are, of course, necessary but they are not the key factors of success. What use are the best technology and a fat budget if the Moscow office is out on the street?

Best Practice has an open mindset. After the Moscow incident, the battered Western company was seething: »Those damned Russians!« A manager with an open mindset, on the other hand, would say: »Man, what went wrong there? Why did *that* happen? What exactly did the Russians do? And what did we do to make them behave like that? How can we stop this from happening again in the future?«

Doing what you know is Best Practice.

Leaders are the ones asking the questions. However, few people actually act on it. What we are talking about here is the so-called knowing-doing gap, as two Harvard professors, Pfeffer and Sutton, would call it: Doing what you know is Best Practice.

As the sales director at a mechanical engineering company once said: »The question is how quickly can our engineers become Chinese?«

How to become Chinese

The foreign market isn't the determining factor. The national submarkets are.

Company managements have now realized that success in a foreign market is not determined by the foreign market: Success in a specific foreign market (for example, mechanical engineering) is not determined by the foreign market but by the national submarkets (real estate, banks, labor, et cetera).

Companies operating outside of Best Practice have great difficulties understanding this. To put it bluntly: If I am a chocolate expert and I want to succeed in the chocolate market, then, of course, I will also need experts in chocolate but, more importantly, experts in real estate, finance, public authorities and administration.

The engineer mentality is now struggling with this realization. Those who are not are currently booking cross-cultural training to get a handle on local submarkets. This is very well intentioned but mostly of little use, as the customary training courses result in very little transfer of ideas. They also cannot prevent further rental disasters in Moscow. You don't believe me?

Let's take a look at what happens at a typical cross-cultural training course. A Belgian company wants to prepare eight managers for its Chinese expansion. It invites a Chinese instructor who tells the Western managers more or less how things work in China. After that, the Western managers go to China and, after twelve months, the performance of their supply chain still ranks at the lower end of the scale. Can you guess why?

It does not help having a Chinese instructor explain China to Western managers. It just goes in one ear and out the other. What else did you expect? Nobody can learn how to play tennis by *listening* to Roger Federer. Best Practice knows this. That is why it doesn't invite one, but six Chinese to it's cross-cultural training. Or one Chinese and one Russian and one Brazilian and one Indian ... and they all come from within the company.

At such events, Westerners do not just listen to the BRICsters. They *practice* together in the seminar what they will need to do together later on as well. For example, they might simulate a purchasing project. During the seminar both the Westerners and the BRICsters misbehave as they normally would. Afterwards, cultural differences are highlighted, analyzed and discussed openly. That is a lot of work. But in the end, the mixed cultural teams will cooperate better and outperform the competition – who still invite Chinese key-note speakers to bore their managers to death for a high charge and low learning effect and do not manage to prevent a Bejing real estate disaster.

This makes clear why Best Practice has the better network pilots: Before network pilots start fighting with an Indian supplier and embarrass themselves hopelessly, they fight with an Indian from their own organization in a role play. The Indians from within the company point out quickly which language they should avoid with

Indian suppliers if they want to prevent expensive delays in supply and incorrect deliveries. The really amazing thing is: Because Best Practice trains with ›real foreigners‹, it realizes savings.

They can only achieve this because they calculate their own way. Board members always say: »I won't fly in employees for training from all over the world. That is way too expensive!« It is a question of price calculation. Best Practice board members calculate differently. They say: »All the traveling adds up to a five-digit figure. But what we save afterwards in negotiations and costs of friction, in missing and defective deliveries, will be millions.« That is total value calculation. Best Practice puts into practice what it wants to train: supply chain management instead of just purchasing. It doesn't calculate with the cost price, not even with total cost, but with total value.

Best Practice managers calculate differently, so they can develop better network leaders.

And this can be calculated down to the last penny, when a good controller comes into the game. A wholesaler from southern Germany once told me: »In Eastern European Country A we are losing 20 cents for each euro because of a whole range of delivery problems. In Eastern European Country B, it is only 7 cents.« Why is that? Because after the bad experiences in Country A, the purchasers got training for Country B with ›real foreigners‹, real tasks and real problems from the supply chain.

Globalization of the management board

What drives up costs for a purchaser can be fatal for the management board.

The world can not be managed from Timbuktu.

A surprisingly high number of Western country board members know their foreign locations from spreadsheets or symposiums like the China Sourcing Summit. Best Practice managers are not as attached to their home turf. They travel a lot.

Think global, act local the rallying cry of globalization.

Take Stephan Biesenbach, for example, CPO of the energy supplier Vattenfall. People say he spends more time in the air than on the ground. If you ask him why he is rushing around the globe like a man possessed, he would throw up his hands in disbelief, wondering how any intelligent person could think you can steer a global supply and distribution network from the comfort of your own home. Or, as Holger Schober, Director of International Executive Education at SMI, likes to say: »The world is globalized, so we have to be as well.«

If the general does not show up regularly to inspect his troops, the troops will go off in a thousand directions.

Anyone not being seen regularly at their sites abroad or visiting their global partners along the supply chain will never understand why Best Practice managers can control their networks so well. The reasons are hierarchical: The local network bosses usually don't have to report to the CPO at headquarters. They report to their own local big boss. CPO Biesenbach is then able to order what he wants from Germany – if the Norwegians do not want to go along with things, they just won't. Unless Biesenbach jets off and gets the Norwegians back on board with his great leadership skills, by finding out their sensitivities and integrating their country-specific particularities, which he would not be able to see from Germany. This is how controlling networks works. That is why we need leaders like Biesenbach. The ancient Romans were also aware of that.

Or as the saying goes: »When the cat's away, the mice will play.«

Company Olympics

The biggest problem in steering networks is the disparity among the countries of the network. It is quite common to have countries which are better than others, with some that are unfortunately a lot worse. The question is: why?

In many companies you have the best rumors circulating around on this: »Mexicans have a big party every Friday!«, »The French have three-hour lunch breaks!« Best Practice managers do not waste time on such rumors. They take advantage of the simple instrument of global projects for measurement.

If all 140 supply chain managers, for example, in all 12 nations are given the same project, you will get a lot more than the usual national ranking out of it. When you look at the different approaches to solving problems in the project, it becomes clear how, where and why the under-performers made mistakes and what were the success factors of the over-performers. In this way you can not only tackle the weaknesses of the weaker countries, you can also lead the weaker to the strengths of the stronger.

When everyone jumps over the same crossbar, you can make out the best jumpers with your naked eyes and the reasons why.

Up until now, it has been predominantly Best Practice managers carrying out such company Olympics. Because they are the only leaders who have realized it is the best way to solve the problem of disparity in different countries.

What companies do to deserve the ›Best Practice‹ label can be seen in the following example.

Best Practice: Deutsche Post DHL

It's obvious that intercultural competence is important to the German company Deutsche Post DHL. The company is the world market leader in logistics. You can travel to the ends of the earth and no matter where you are – you will always find a DHL delivery truck on its way. This world wide presence however is a great challenge for Deutsche Post DHL and especially for its employees. In order to make its employees fit for procurement all over the world, the company's purchasing department developed a training program entitled »Fit4Procurement«:

Fitness for procurement employees

- Training locations:
  Bad Honnef, Bangkok, Bedford, Beijing, Brussels, Fort Lauderdale, Hong Kong, Jakarta, Kuala Lumpur, Manila, Lahnstein, Mexico City, Mumbai, Sao Paulo, Seoul, Shanghai, Chenzhen, Siegburg, Singapore, Stockholm, Sydney, Taipeh, Tokyo, Fellberst-Langenberg
- Training staff:
  Approx. one dozen internal trainers

- Scope:
  Approx. 90 seminars for around 600 participants with 170 seminars and 1,500 participant days
- Annual performance:
  59 training programs in 564 training locations
- Contents:
  From ›Successful Marketing of Procurement Services‹ to Sourcing and Supply and Project Management and Contract Management

The first thing you will notice in this chart is, of course, the training locations: Think global, act local. That means: lots of training locations in lots of different countries. Those who immediately think about all the different languages spoken there have already recognized an important part of the problem. However, training is not the only area in the global networks where more than one language is spoken.

Now you speak my language

When in Rome, do as the Romans do.

»When in Rome, do as the Romans do«, the English like to say. »Different countries, different behaviours«, say the Germans. These sayings hold a very bitter truth for networks: Country-specific differences in the understanding of working processes are decisive in the success of networks.

A working process in Kenya has to be handled just as carefully and efficiently as it would in England. This is the dangerous thing about global networks. A network's performance which is first class in 15 different countries in the world can damage the entire network because of a foul-up in just one of the countries. The employee in charge of that particular network was – well, having a bad day? Or, more likely, took a more relaxed view and does not define or carry out working processes in quite the same way as his colleagues in the other 15 countries.

This means that all the crosspoints on a global network should apply the same management tools, for example, the same cost analysis tools and instruments for supplier management, and share the same awareness and understanding of the processes. Regardless of which country in the world, future suppliers should be required to comply with the same quality criteria. And they definitely are not yet able to. Not because the suppliers in emerging countries »are not that far along yet«. Although this can matter, it is not the decisive factor.

The most crucial factor can be demonstrated more clearly with this example of a food corporation: Supply managers check their potential new suppliers in 15 countries by visiting them in person. The 16th country merely looks at the supplier's paperwork without having a look around. Because of this carelessness, the employee could have a few problems. But the problems occuring in the network will be a lot worse because the poorly selected suppliers in the 16th country will bring down not only that country, but the others in the network as well.

That is the domino effect of global networks – everything is linked. And if the countries in this network do not all speak the same language, you will soon have a language chaos similar to that of ancient Babylon. And that does not just apply to the ›language of networks‹ in work processes. It also applies to the language that is spoken in the network which is usually English. Surprisingly, however, it does not work.

English does not work!

English is the corporate language at the above-mentioned company. And elsewhere as well. But elsewhere there is no training. That is why it does not work. How can that be? English is supposed to be *the* international language! At least that is what they say in books. But reality looks different.

It does not even work between two native English speaking nations. Whenever Brits talk to Americans (whether in a business or political context) the words they use to talk about each other *afterwards* are not fit to print here. They just do not understand each other!

In Japan it is considered unrefined to speak English. The Chinese do not understand what the actual meaning is, and the Germans get more wrong than right of what is actually being said. In a globalized world these are the conditions within which you are supposed to have a civilized conversation *and* solve mutual problems effectively. Keep dreaming.

English only works as a corporate language after (intensive) training.

Once again, this is so obvious that, so far, only Best Practice can summon up the necessary courage, budget, programs, and control mechanisms to actually implement something so obvious. The troubles with this particular triviality explain another problem that many companies are also ignoring. This one is even more unpleasant. Or do you like trouble?

Trouble in the network

Conflict within networks is the status quo.

After only a few minutes of talking with a network manager, I'll have heard six anecdotes about something that »the Indians«, »the Americans«, or »the Germans« have done again. These testimonies to mutual dislike are circulated as enthusiastically as jokes about blondes or politicians. It is not that there is anything fundamentally wrong with telling jokes. Within networks they are more a symptom than a disease:

Which is not such a bad thing, really. In every good marriage, conflict is a necessary evil. It does not mean something is wrong, it is just an unavoidable part of it. It only becomes dangerous when you are no longer able to deal with these natural, normal everyday occurrences because the two partners lack a basic understanding of each other.

»We are not talking to the Yanks anymore,« said an Italian designer in a multinational corporation. »We supply them with our latest designs and instead of being grateful they complain. We naturally ignore their complaints and simply send them new models. We keep doing this until they give up. Good design always wins out in the end.« But unfortunately, it does not sell.

At least not in America. That is what the ›Yanks‹ have been trying to tell the Italians for the last three years. So far they haven't succeeded. For three years the product line has been sitting on the supermarket shelves. You wonder how much longer the corporation can afford this poorly selling product line which isn't due to the product being bad or a slump in demand. It is because your own people cannot communicate with each other. Why not?

Conflict training is not designed to strengthen your conflict skills, it is to show your colleagues that you are not able to manage your conflicts on your own! This at least is the prevailing attitude. That is why conflicts in your own country are more or less tolerated rather than mediated. When other nationalities are concerned, the conflict potential will increase exponentially.

International networks only function with international conflict management.

The above mentioned company realized this and implemented resolute international conflict management training. This is paying off. In the food corporation's network the susceptibility, intensity and duration of conflicts is significantly lower than in other networks. Not because the employees get on better with each other or because they are one big happy family. It is because they have better conflict management tools to use if conflicts do flare up. Even better – before they flare up. If you have the right tools, you can deal better with conflicts. Which is not the end of the story. Most managers have access to good conflict management tools. They just don't use them.

Most managers have access to good conflict management tools. They just don't use them.

Why not? This is a mystery which psychologists around the world have been trying to solve. The Harvard professors Pfeffer and Sutton even wrote a book about it: *The Knowing-Doing Gap.* Some people know so much and use their knowledge so little. Why is that? I do not know the answer to that question, but there is one thing I do know: If you train your knowledge, you will increase your knowledge. If you train applying your knowledge, you will also apply what you have learned!

Why is training carried out in so many companies without the chance to put it into practice? I think some people believe: »It'll sort itself out!« But it won't: Conflicts develop their own momentum. Every system continues to move in the direction it was pushed. This is important as international conflict management can only be learned by managing international conflicts, with the help of an experienced coach.

Network harmony

Global networks have to be harmonized. That's the key to efficiency.

Of course, all the countries in the global network are working together one way or another. Unfortunately, »one way or another« is not good enough.

When cooperation in the network is unsystematic and without order, with everyone working to their own definition of processes and standards, it quickly degenerates into chaos, which is the state most networks are currently in. Networks have to be harmonized. How would you go about achieving that?

If you want to establish global standards, you will have to train locally. Think global, act local.

Random network harmonization is nothing more than a joke, which is easily pushed aside by the mechanisms which rule the markets. Unfortunately, too many companies are being taken in by this joke. They have the motto: The orders come from Düsseldorf (or Vienna, New York, Beijing ...) – and the world should take note! A sad misapprehension. The fact that our food manufacturer did not succumb to this can be seen by the number of their seminar locations, which are at a fair distance from the headquarters in Milan. Training is carried out in almost every country in the world where the corporation is located. The simple reasoning behind it: If you want to establish global standards, you will have to train locally. Think global, act local.

The concept was central, the training local, and the goal unimodal: harmonization. Only a harmonized network is an effective and efficient network.

Why is the harmonization of networks outside of Best Practice so notoriously difficult? The answer is simple: It is all in the structure.

Welcome to the Radical Structuralism Club!

The structure defines the process and therefore the result.

How many bars of gold can you fit into a beer bottle? A silly question, of course: none! Even if you melted the bars – the bottle would melt, too. Bars do not fit into bottles. Or put another way: The structure (the bottle) defines the process and therefore the result.

You can work yourself to death, hiring the best people and the most expensive consultants – if the structure isn't right, the result is poppycock. Garbage in, garbage out, right?

Networks are no monoculture.

It is actually even worse than that. The wrong structure can cause damage. Or as a board member once assured me: »If you put gold into a shredder, it still comes out in useless shards.« This merciless aside beautifully describes the fruitless endeavors of many companies trying to harmonize the international centrifugal forces of their networks: As hard as they try, nothing much comes out of it – because they are using the wrong structure. A structure that is central, monocultural and directing. Headquarters demands harmonization – and that is exactly what cannot be achieved.

The Argentinians are delivering contaminated filets? Then the Italians will have to bring those Argentinians back into line! How do the Argentinians react? They continue to deliver rotten meat ... Globalization is based on archaic, neurotic and supremely human mechanisms. Quel surpris.

Except that the food corporation was not taken by ›surpris‹. They knew how important structure is for the result they wanted and chose a multicultural, multifunctional structure. It wasn't the Italians who told the Argentinians to improve hygiene, it was someone from the local Argentinian organization. It wasn't a chemist either, but an expert in production lines. The food corporation also structured the organization of a task force for network harmonization correctly, too. The task force reported immediately to the CPO, to avoid the formation of yet another working circle which could be more or less ignored by everybody else.

The right harmonization structure means the right harmonization result.

It is definitely possible to fail even before you have really begun: By choosing the wrong structure. Conversely, anyone can be assured of success before they have actually begun: By choosing the right structure.

At a glance: Do not conquer the world, understand it

- Cross-cultural competence continues to be underestimated.
- Companies most frequently fail in foreign markets because they do not know the local submarkets such as real estate, banking, administration, etc.
- Tip: In foreign markets it is not the best product or the biggest budget which wins but the best knowledge of the local submarkets.
- Tip: You cannot manage global networks professionally from head office. You have to visit them. Think global, act local.
- Tip: Cross-border corporate Olympics are ideal for internal benchmarking as well as learning from the best.

6 The secret of champions

»Lighting a cigarette only looks cool when you've done it a thousand times before.«
Humphrey Bogart

The Buffett effect

Who is the best investor in the world? Warren Buffett. Who is the best golfer? Tiger Woods. Why are they the best?

We usually know who the best person in a particular discipline is; there are world rankings and the Olympics for this. Only a few people know, however, *why* the best are the best.

It is easier to make your employees fitter when you know what makes the best so much better.

For thousands of years, people have been admiring Olympic athletes, champions and other winners. And in these thousands of years, humanity as a whole has never figured out *why* Buffett is Buffett or discovered the secret of champions. For most of us, that is okay. It is not the end of the world if we cannot all be a Woods, Federer or Miller. We have got our jobs, after all, and we do not necessarily need an Olympic medal. For the average citizen this is a perfectly acceptable knowledge gap. For a manager, however, it can be a catastrophe.

No one really knows exactly? Is it a secret? On the contrary. It is no secret, it is a surprise!

The specificity of a winner

Buffett, Federer, Woods, Navratilova, Graf, the Williams sisters, Schumacher … How can you explain such high performance? »Natural talent«, »genius«, »it is in their genes«, you say. That is so off the mark, it makes me wonder why people play golf at all if they obviously don't learn anything from it.

When I play golf, the following phenomenon occurs more regularly than the sun shines: Amateurs come out of their golf lessons and meander through the course on their way to the club house. They complain to each other jovially, »My swing is a mess. Mine goes too far to the right. I am just not hitting far enough ...« What would a professional say?

He wouldn't say anything. Because he is still on the green, practicing his swing. And I do not just mean that the best practice longer. That is obvious, of course they train longer. The point I am trying to make was explained to me by a management board member who was lucky enough to watch two national team soccer players practicing at the last World Championship games. One of them was Brazilian.

The board member came too late to practice because he had been stuck in a traffic-jam. He only managed to see one of the Brazilians kicking the ball casually around. He complained to his companion, »Man, I missed the best part. They're obviously just doing their cool down.« His companion turned to him with a smile and said, »This *is* the training! They've been kicking the ball around like that the whole time. Doing tricks and showing off.« No need to say that it was another one of those world championships where the best players in the world didn't become the world champions. Why not?

The answer came to the board member during the second training session he witnessed. He just did not understand the answer. And he did not try to hide it during a round of Martinis: »I just don't understand! They didn't practice game tactics or plays to use against the opposing team. They only practiced double passes, free kicks and pushing the ball forward. They only practiced the trivial things over and over again. They are the best soccer players in the world and they only practice easy stuff like that? Shouldn't they have mastered those things a long time ago?«

That is a pretty tragical mistake a lot of people make: World championships are not won by the team with the best ›game plan‹, or the ›best tactics‹, or the team which has adapted their defense appropriately enough for the opposing team. The champions are the ones who make the game-winning goals. Tactics are great. Scoring goals is better. So teams should practice exactly the things which are specific to success.

The best are the best because they train specifically.

Hundreds of actors have tried to light a cigarette as coolly and confidently as Humphrey Bogart. And most of them seemed pretty awkward when they did. Because Bogart was a genius at lighting cigarettes? When Bogey heard that, he supposedly laughed, and answered with the same message we are trying to get across here: »Lighting a cigarette only looks cool when you've done it a thousand times before.« The copycats look so awkward because they haven't practiced with the same specific obsession as the master. If they had, they would have become legends as well. At least in lighting cigarettes.

Best Practice trains what other people are too ›good‹ for: specificity.

I caught one of the best network managers I know studying transport agreements. I teased him by asking, »You concern yourself with such banalities?« He couldn't understand and said, »What may look like a banality to you is the basis of success to me.«

It is as easy as that. I never said that the recipe for Best Practice was complex, difficult or highly academic. It is not those things, and that is why it works.

Why just them?

Money down the drain

In Best Practice, network managers are being trained specifically. Most others do not know what specificity means. Many believe their employees have already been trained very specifically, even though the opposite is true. The CPO of an investment goods manufacturer believed this as well. Over the course of the latest crisis, he experienced a continuous loss of suppliers in his global network.

»Our supply chain managers must learn to recognize sooner if a supplier is on shaky ground!«, he said in a note of urgency to his personnel department. They immediately booked a negotiation training seminar so their purchasers and network managers would be able to tell more easily and quickly during negotiations whether a candidate was operating on shaky ground. Three weeks after the end of the seminar, yet another supplier surprised everyone by going bust. The CPO yelled at his people, »You've all been doing role-play exercises to get ready for precisely this situation, and you still cannot do it? Why am I wasting funds from our tight budget on your training if you don't learn anything from it?« In response to this, one of his best people stood up and gave him his opinion, which turned out to be a real stroke of luck for the CPO.

In spite of vast sums spent on training still not a champion?

The high-potential employee said, »Hey boss, you book the wrong training for us and then blame us when anything goes wrong? No offense, but if I talk with my suppliers about a disturbing situation, do you really think that they're going to just admit it, right off the bat? They come back at me with the 20 standard excuses. If I only knew how to probe into each of these 20 excuses so I could disprove them, then I could get rid of the rotten apples. Yes, we role-played negotiations until we dropped in that training, but guess what? Not a single one of the 20 relevant excuses was covered!« Why not?

Because the trainer didn't know them – which is only logical. He does not work 5 days a week buying parts for valve systems that cool atomic plants or valves for heart and lung machines and then listen to the specific excuses the suppliers have to offer. If this is such a clear and obvious fact, then why did the CPO hire an ignorant trainer? Was he acting carelessly? Not at all. Neither was the trainer ›ignorant‹. Both were suffering from a widely held misconception about specificity:

The abstract is not just specific.

The CPO thought that if his people learned in an abstract way to use open-ended questions (instead of using closed yes-or-no questions) when probing for answers, they could then use this abstract principle to formulate specific, open-ended questions with which they could dig deeper into a supplier's claim that all of his delays in delivery were ›only a stock problem‹. Yet it is exactly this assumption of knowledge transfer that isn't correct. It is never correct. Would the correct open-ended question spontaneously occur to you?

Specific questions have to be developed specifically first, and under no circumstances by participants in the training seminar itself (they can't, otherwise they wouldn't be sitting in the training course). This makes clear why up until now only Best Practice has trained specifically: The cross-over from theoretical jargon to concrete specificity is really hard work.

The cross-over from theoretical jargon to concrete specificity is really hard work.

It is detective work.

Detective work

The manufacturer of investment goods would be training his network managers specifically if he trained the 20 specific questions they needed to ask when their suppliers tried to give their 20 favourite excuses. Finding these questions requires detective work, so the CPO engaged a new negotiations trainer with network experience to act as a detective for him.

This time, the CPO asked the trainer to begin with the detective work long before the actual training session was scheduled to begin, and this is precisely what the fellow did. Together with their individual supervisors he selected 15 from a possible 70 participants. This alone took half a day because they wanted to choose those participants who not only thought things through well but who could also express themselves well (give good answers to the detective's questions).

The trainer then gathered these 15 employees and went through the 20 most common excuses used by suppliers. He investigated the most common questions and their effect which resulted in the Best Practice method of handling excuses. Subsequently he gathered some communications experts and a specialist for supply chain risk management and analyzed the best questioning strategies, formulating additional questions and developing model phrases. They were tested by the 15 carefully selected employees on real suppliers in practical testing situations. The result of the exercise was a list of 20 conversation models for dealing with excuses that proved effective in shooting down 80 percent of all excuses.

It was exactly these 20 conversation models that were then trained for one day. Five days of specific detective work were necessary for this single day of training. As a result of this training session, the valve manufacturer's competition claimed (with no small amount of alarm) that the valve manufacturer »must have their ears to the ground.« They reduced the number of their ›supply chain surprises‹ from ten a month to two, because their supply chain managers can now ›sense‹ a supplier's impending insolvency quicker than all the others in the field.

If that is so easy, why isn't everybody doing it? Because they can't.

Not anyone can do it

The specificity of a winner can never be brought into a company if the manager in charge lacks awareness. This lack of understanding is clearly identified by signature phrases like, »I am not going to train my employees in such obvious things! They should know that by now, they do it every day!« Yes, of course they *should* already know it ...

But they cannot do it any better than the soccer millionaires can, who should definitely already be able to. Is it because both are unmotivated and slow learners? No, it is because our Western system of education is much too abstract. Why are the graduates of private business universities so much better? Because they are educated in a much more specific manner, much closer to reality. If your employees are qualified, but too non-specific, you shouldn't blame them. You should blame our highly-praised educational system.

Why will you never hear a Best Practice manager uttering phrases like, »But my people should already know how to do that«? Because they have awareness. They know that the key to success is specificity, and they think in specific terms rather than abstract concepts. They have an unerring eye for details like great generals always had. It is said that Napoleon, for example, when passing a battery of seven canons at a distance of 50 meters, could immediately notice if one of the fuse caps was sticking out by even 1 centimeter.

Best Practice managers are competent in processes.

Normally, these essential details are specific business processes, such as checking out the excuses most commonly used by suppliers. That, too, is a Best Practice ability: Best Practice managers are competent in processes.

Doesn't that go without saying? Not really. To adapt Henry Mintzberg loosely, »We spend most of our lifetime with business processes, but only very few of us actually understand them.« Even if the understanding is there, up to now only in Best Practice there is money spent on it.

Which company would pay a trainer not to train, but instead, to wander around the firm asking employees questions about the 20 most common excuses used by suppliers? Only Best Practice companies do. And to be honest, paying a trainer is not even the biggest problem. First you have to find one who can do it!

Most trainers are ›just‹ that – trainers. They are not field researchers who question employees in a reliable, valid and representative way and then develop an effective training concept. This means that Best Practice companies do not only have top managers with the necessary amount of specificity awareness. They do not only come up with funding for the necessary detective work. They are also so good at selecting trainers that they identify the field researchers among them and hire them at reasonable prices.

To find out what else Best Practice is able to do, let's take another look at concrete – sorry, *specific* – examples.

Best Practice: United States Postal Services

The United States Postal Services (USPS) is an independent company owned by the US government which distributes more mail to more addresses in one of the largest regional postal areas than any other postal service in the world: Its 660,000 employees process 46 percent of all the postcards and letters sent out. Their turnover amounts to around 75 billion dollars (2008). 430 purchasers and asset management professionals spend more than 13 billion dollars with 25,000 suppliers.

Supply chain management at USPS saw their remit, recently, the same as all well-managed companies: Ensuring that their employees get fitter in their jobs to be able to manage the USPS supply network even more effectively and efficiently, reducing expenditure even more fiercely in a time of immense cost pressures, and teasing out even more efficiency and innovative potentials from their suppliers. And there you have the entire hidden difficulty in a nutshell: What does ›increased efficiency‹ really mean? What does ›reducing costs‹ mean? There are many programs on cost reduction and increasing efficiency, that all have similar names and are similarly ineffective. But why?

It is not because employees aren't pulling their weight. Or because the market is changing too quickly. It is because the task is so unspecific that any average person would be programmed to fail. And still, less successful companies often proclaim this kind of unspecific programs.

USPS is different. The postmasters charged immediately ahead to confront their task specific deficit, leaving that unspecific program jingle echoing in the dust: »What's the advantage of having the best employees,« asked Susan Brownell, Vice President of Supply Management, »if they're going to leave the company anyway?« A typical Best Practice problem: Your employees are good. They are so good that they are in strong demand, not only in your company.

This is why USPS had to, and wanted to, develop their supply management professionals into the best, as well as finding a way to hold on to them – and from the beginning they would not only hire the best, but offer them programs to ensure they were more likely to stay. The result was a comprehensive program developed by the management which consisted of three main parts we are going to consider in detail:

- Recruitment: Who wants to be a supply management professional?
- Development: The virtual supply chain management academy.
- Retention: Rotating is remaining

Recruitment: Who wants to be a supply management professional?

In 2006, USPS faced a big problem: For every newly recruited employee two others left the company. It takes no Albert Einstein to figure out where this would lead to. What should companies do in this situation? What would you do?

The standard knee-jerk reaction is to pump up the budget for recruitment advertisements, pay employees above average and start an expensive image campaign. Will that help? Not really. It is too unspecific.

The relationship between cause and effect is specific. You just have to recognize it.

What goes for ›management‹ these days may appear strange. Reacting to a massive manpower exodus with an image campaign is nothing less than presumptuous – or a camouflaged cry for help. The hypothesis behind this image campaign seems clear: It is completely or mostly due to our image that we have fewer candidates applying than needed. That could well be possible. Deciding on the cause, however, without any analysis is guesswork, which is then raised to the level of universal truth. This is the Pope's job. And according to the latest survey, he is no member of the management.

Some will simply react out of a need for action: »Too few applicants? Well then we'll have to pimp our advertising!« That is ambitious and challenging, but not effective because it isn't specific. Picking the most likely from all possible causes of problems and then throwing a budget at it does not require a manager. A random generator can do it for you. It is just as unspecific.

The USPS management went about it in a specific way. The company first set up a project team to find out the true, specific reasons for the lack of applicants. They were baffling indeed. Intense research and benchmarking activities soon showed that it had nothing to do at all with the company's image. USPS was considered an attractive employer and the advertised positions offered interesting tasks, good pay, and excellent career prospects. Even so, conspicuously few candidates were applying. The project group dug deeper and found the reason for this reluctance. Can you guess?

It is a very common phenomenon in modern network management (because modern network management is not as modern in its administrative setup as it is in its actual performance). The reason was that the world's universities are still not educating enough supply management professionals and, more importantly, that the highly complex description of the advertised positions confused even the bravest of applicants. This is what the USPS project group found out. What did management do about it? They sorted out half of the usual requirements and then just left them out.

In this way – and with the help of a few other measures – they managed a turnaround for the company: Within two years, their churn rate was only half. For each person leaving a new employee was hired. The recruitment rate increased from 5.5 percent to 9.6 percent – in relation to the entire workforce in purchasing.

It is certainly popular to take care of the ›unspecific‹ in the market with job offers, headhunters and image campaigns because it has an aura of action. But it is too unspecific to be effective, not only useless, but even harmful. It makes companies waste more and more money on the wrong applicants. Some companies are developing an unwanted reputation in the industry. They even know it. Yet they do not seem to realize the true reason for their personnel misery: their unbridled randomness in recruitment.

Development: The Virtual Supply Chain Academy

Three guesses which measures USPS used in their personnel development. You got it! The company founded its own Supply Chain Academy. You might dismiss it as just another management trend. I consider it a must for success-oriented companies.

A Corporate Procurement University (CPU) is pretty much as specific as you can get in developing network managers. No ›off the shelf‹ programs, just training which clearly shows the specificity in the program description itself. CPU programs are custom-made for companies and activities (otherwise they don't deserve the CPU label – which unfortunately is much too rare.)

USPS's idea of starting up their own academy for supply chain management was admittedly nothing new. What is surprising about the USPS University is that it is completely virtual. And it works! That is truly amazing.

While Europe is still doing its best to get to grips with e-learning, America is charging ahead as leader of the global pack. How the Americans got the e-academy set up is worth mentioning, especially if you consider the advantages of such a virtual campus:

- E-academy offers immense savings on budget costs, opportunity costs, time and CO_2-emissions – because no one has to travel.
- Unlike all other types of training, it is available 24 hours a day, 7 days a week.
- The training is unusually flexible: everyone trains when they have the time (and, more importantly, when they feel like it).
- E-learning can offer many more programs than a ›presence-based‹ concept.

At USPS, for example, employees can choose from over 300 different types of training related to supply chain management – from general business practice to the entire purchasing and supply chain specific categories, including asset management.

If you take a look around now, you'll see a lot of hands raised and waving frantically. They all belong to those hollering: »E-learning? It does not work! Not for us!«

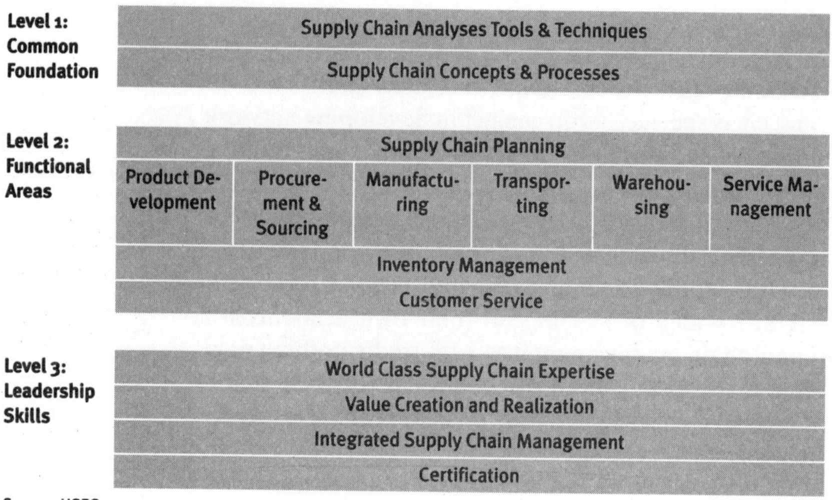

Source: USPS

Figure 11: USPS Supply Chain Academy Program

This reminds me of a neighbor who recently moved into a new home. The movers had to carry a piano to the third floor. One of them sat down at the keyboard after their work was done and tried to produce something akin to a melody. When he realized he failed he asked: »Which keys do you have to press to play some music? This widget doesn't work at all!«

No wiser words have ever been spoken about the internet, too: If you're trying to do something really useful, it doesn't work!

The internet doesn't work!

In the early days of the internet, an inexperienced computer nerd had the glorious idea that such a ubiquitous medium would be perfect for training, and above all suitable for the global net: Networks are spread all over the world, and the only existing medium which can network in realtime, acoustically, and visually with practically no extra costs is the internet. That was the birth of e-learning 2.0. Everything was there: the technology, the possibilities, the network. Only people were once again refusing to cooperate.

If an employee is given the chance to learn in a modern way at his very own personal computer and the possibility to gain new qualifications which will help him and his company to improve their human capital, increase their productivity and expand their network – or to surf, chat and look at pictures in the internet, it is a no-brainer. Anyone attending an e-academy program under these circumstances would have to be crazy. Millions are being spent for e-learning programs which only a few people really use.

Marketing for educational programs is as important as the educational programs themselves.

At USPS, however, within the first six months of their web-based supply chain academy, more than 90 percent of all employees in purchasing and supply chain management had not only taken one course, but four or more. You are green with envy? No surprise if you consider the undeniable fact that some companies have not even managed to get their workforce to even click on their e-academy's homepage. What are the Americans doing differently?

It is no coincidence that USPS is an American company: The US are the promised land when it comes to marketing.

Marketing can save the world

That it had to be an American company, of all things, to achieve the most successful e-learning program is in blatant contrast to the leading world-wide training philosophy which can be summed up in just three words: Content is king.

Most managers, trainers and teachers have made this motto their religion. The CPO of a Spanish food manufacturer recently told me with unabashed pride that their project team of HR experts, network pilots, external trainers, and representatives from individual departments had spent, believe it or not, eight months working on the conception of their procurement university – the conception of their program content, notabene. Three months after the opening celebrations, however, the academy turned out to be ›not as successful as expected‹. Six months later it was more or less forgotten because it had never achieved acceptance. It was lacking the support of individual departments and the managers in purchasing. Memo to the CPO: What's the use of nobel prize worthy content if nobody takes notice?

Americans are better protected against this widespread faux pas than any other nation: They wouldn't package a single item without a marketing strategy. In plain words: USPS didn't just launch an intranet platform for e-learning, in fact they didn't launch one at all beforehand. First they launched a marketing campaign that could have competed with any Hollywood blockbuster.

The offices of the 430 potential academy students, that means network management employees, were decorated with larger than life posters proclaiming in flashy type:

Attention!

Coming soon to a personal computer near you:
The Supply Chain Academy!

The semantic resemblance to a movie release is obvious and did not fall short of its mark: The potential cinemagoers sat in tremulous anticipation at their desks, awaiting the ›movie premiere‹. Are you getting the picture?

Then your ancestors must have been Americans because outside of America most CPOs are already turning up their noses: The top network boss as carneval barker and cinema showman? Susan Brownell, Vice President of Supply Management, has a more pragmatic view: »Well, of course! If it helps to fill up the academy vacancies ... Our philosophy is: whatever it takes.«

It is always the same: Specificity wins. And the specific shortcoming of a Corporate Procurement University is neither the content nor the crew of instructors, it is the acceptance (or lack of it) by potential attendants, hierarchies and bosses. If employees feel that training is a burden or that they have to pay for some mistake they made in the past, they'll fight against it tooth and nail – or torpedo the transfer. If attending the academy is as hip and cool as the latest Will Smith movie, then they'll queue to get in. And they will only

SCA Peak Performance Contest	
VP's 15-day Challenge	**Monthly Challenge**
Requirements: • Have access to SCA • Complete one SCA course by July 12th	**Requirements:** • Have access to SCA • Complete four SCA courses during one month
Recognition: • Automatically entered into a Random Drawing • Automatically entered into the Honorable Mention Club • One employee will receive a $25 certificate	**Recognition:** • Automatically entered into a Random Drawing • Automatically entered into the Honorable Mention Club • Three employees will receive a $25 certificate **FY 2008 Contest Dates:** • June 23 – July 31 Drawing August 1st • August 1 – August 31 Drawing September 1st • Sept. 1 – Sept. 30 Drawing October 1st

Source: USPS

Figure 12: Advertisement of USPS Supply Chain Academy

keep on coming if the movie gets rave reviews. There are more good films no one ever saw because of bad marketing than films you wished you had never seen.

Every CPU needs a first class marketing program.

First class means: multimedia-based. In addition to posters, the Americans bombarded their target group with voice mails, webcasts, videos and even a competition – with anything, in effect, an average US consumer is used to if a new product is being launched. If the new supermarket around the corner opens to a huge hullabaloo, a sensible CPO shouldn't announce his brand new academy like rotting leftovers with an internal memo. Not even in Europe. It doesn't work and makes it seem ridiculous, as if the CPO wasn't really interested in his employees developing their skills to a new level. Fortunately, European CPOs are normally more progressive than I like to admit: at least those who are open to Best Practice.

Recently, a purchaser from a large retailer told me full of excitement that his new boss had cycled around the hallways of his department for half a day with the announcement of a new training program in his hand – on a unicycle. Certainly, the man used to be a triathlete and was quite athletic. Anyway, hats off! In his department (and in the entire company) everyone is still talking about his publicity stunt. And: The training was completely booked two hours after the cycling, plus 37 people on the waiting list.

Retention: Rotating is remaining

We are getting closer to the crux of the matter: USPS actually managed to get more and better candidates to apply. They managed to make them even better with the help of the e-academy. There's still one question left unanswered: How does the company make sure the well-selected and well-trained employees stay at USPS?

First USPS gave employees the chance to work from a home office and/or use flexi-time. That may be widespread in Europe, but in America it is still the exception to the rule: Most people still live up to the song Dolly Parton once sang, »working nine to five«.

Develop leaders! And keep them!

For particularly important high potentials and leaders, the company introduced a program of job rotation. Every person selected had to go through at least three different areas. Just a little reminder: Job rotation is commonly recognized as one of the cornerstones of activity in the workplace and of worker satisfaction. No one wants to work 24/7 in the same old routine. Or as the Americans say: »Same old, same old.«

Job rotation is nevertheless still quite uncommon. Normally, leaders are motivated to stay through excellent career prospects, salary, premiums, bonuses, company cars and status symbols. But Sprenger has changed that: these things do not really motivate, and definitely not for long. Of course, one will take any bonus the boss is handing out. But at least three weeks later one will find the same old routine about as exciting as before – because apart from the bonus nothing really changed! If one has to continue with the same old job, no bonus in the world can keep one's mood and productivity at a peak level. Does that mean one is spoiled? Exactly. Just like the rest of the leaders. You cannot keep them in companies by offering nothing but the bonus carrot.

Creating employee loyalty begins before the employee joins the company.

An alarming number of employees report that they felt disoriented in their first few weeks in the job. They spend around four days just trying to figure out where their desk is. Then they spend four weeks trying to figure out what their actual work is – while busy personnel within a two-floor radius bombard them with unrequested favors and errands. We all know what it's like. But only few realize that even in working relationships the first impression is incredibly important. Those starting with a cold shower will never really warm up to their employer – and will leave the company more often as a consequence. Especially if they are high potentials.

For this reason, USPS implemented a ›welcome on board‹ program. The ›newbies‹ are mentored by an experienced employee so they will not only find their desk more quickly, they are also introduced systematically into the standard working processes with the possibility to ask questions when necessary.

All in all, USPS is an illustrative example of the usual problems that captains of industry and network managers love to complain about, yet are by no means unsolvable as long as they are handled specifically. This is the cue: If you deal with things without being specific, you can try dozens of remedies and still end up back where you started. If you take care to be specific, you will normally get it right the first time. That's the beauty of specificity.

At a glance: What the best do better

- The best train precisely those details and specific processes that others take for granted or consider too ordinary.
- Tip: The more specific a fitness program is, the better your people will become.
- People cannot transfer things which they have learned abstractly to their actual work. Yet it is demanded by many managers, trainers and HR developers.

- It is a lot of work to identify these details and process components and then prepare them to be trained. Best Practice goes this extra mile.
- Tip: For the successful implementation of a corporate university, education marketing is just as important as the training program.

7 Get a coach!

»Isn't it crazy? We envy the rich, the beautiful and the successful, but we seldom ask ourselves how they made it.«
Charles Handy

The way to success

Imagine that everything went wrong. The banking system falls apart. The GDP falls by 20 percent. Your partner asks you to take her out to dance next Saturday. (Female readers, please use the analogy of a soccer game.) Catastrophe! You know you cannot dance. What can you do?

Coaching is the way to success.

Signing up for a dance class won't help much; it would take weeks before you could even begin to dance like Fred Astaire. If you want to meet a certain challenge as soon as possible you will have to take private lessons or, in modern lingo, get a coach. Most top managers have a coach, just like all top sports stars do. Heidi Klum has her David Kirsch and professional sports teams have motivational trainers. Is this just a passing fad or could there really be something to it? In theory and in practice, coaching is currently considered the way to success, the turbocharger of personal development, and the secret remedy of the very best.

No other tool can cause dramatic changes and boost your abilities faster, more nicely and more effectively. Take Marcel R, for example. He is the head of purchasing in a process technique company. For two years now, he has actually been doing the job of a CPO, but without the official title and the pay that goes with it. For months, he has been complaining to his boss about it, without success. One day he hired an executive coach.

After only two coaching sessions, Marcel could argue his case so convincingly that his boss finally changed his opinion on the matter – an opinion that he had held with inert stubbornness for two long years. After four coaching sessions, Marcel carried out negotiations for his new contract as CPO. He is thrilled about it. What about you? Did you figure out the point of this story?

The point reveals itself by a simple calculation. Without coaching, Marcel would still be the head of purchasing, like many other heads of purchasing. He would still be suffering because he couldn't educate his employees to be the best network pilots possible, because his boss wouldn't approve of the necessary resources – for instance the creation of a supply chain university (see chapter 9) – because Marcel is ›only‹ the head of purchasing and does not wield the required hierarchical weight to push such a university forward. And now to the point: It was not until Marcel happened to pay for career coaching and then became CPO that his company suddenly and surprisingly got the network university they had desperately needed. Now they can train their network pilots to meet the ever-growing demands of globalization. The experts are puzzled: The best network pilots are not a concrete expression of the normative power of company strategy; they are just a by-product, a coincidence, the side effect of a manager just happening to get career coaching at his own cost!

Executive coaching has been around for 30 years, but up to now only high-flying managers have taken advantage of it.

You could now postulate that the world population couldn't care less about the convoluted reasons behind the lack of appropriate training for those who steer global networks as long as they get it one way or the other. However, this is precisely the point. Marcel R. is the exception that proves the rule: Executive coaching has been around for 30 years, but up until now, only a few managers have taken advantage of it. Most of them were high-flying managers.

This means that the networks of the world are wobbling and shaking because a lot of managers are ›too good‹ for coaching.

That is of course debatable. In reality, managers have never been ›too good‹ for coaching.

Help! Here comes the coach!

Why would no respectable manager ever visit a coach? Because it is just psychobabble. As we all know, a coach just wants to prove that at the age of two we pooped outside the pottie and have been dragging a borderline Oedipus complex complete with schizoid attacks of recurrent paranoia (or something like that) around with us ever since.

For 30 years now, the few high-flying managers who actually worked with a coach have been amused by these prejudices. Over the past few months, their smug laughter has been quietly dying away, because coaching is experiencing an unexpected boom and prejudices against it are disappearing as fast as car dealerships. Why?

After 30 years suddenly a boom.

Because the gossip has died down. People say that a good executive coach wouldn't recognize an Oedipus complex if it jumped up and bit him. It makes sense because he is no psychotherapist – otherwise he'd be called one. Even if he could identify an Oedipus complex he would ignore it because a coach is not interested in such things. There is a simple reason for it: No top manager would pay him several hundred euros an hour to do so! The mass dissemination of this trivial realization explains the phenomenon currently being observed: 30 years after its invention, executive coaching is suddenly experiencing a boom.

Coaching also launches a manager and his company into a position of network leadership.

The current boom is also being strengthened by a kind of bandwagon effect. »Lately, almost every manager knows another manager who is experiencing impressive success because of coaching,« says a coach who has been working with managers at all levels in the hierarchy for many years. »People are starting to talk to their colleagues about it. If a trusted colleague has had a good experience with a coach, his recommendation counts for more than a purely rational argument, so it makes you want to try it, too.« This leads to the paradox effect described here: Executive coaching can make a manager's career really take off. The side effect is that coaching also launches a manager and his company into a position of network leadership.

Best Practice was the first to recognize this side effect in all its glory of effectiveness and quickly forge a new leadership tool that works even when worse comes to worst in networks. Worse than a devalued dollar, worse than shrinking sources of raw materials, the absolute worst thing that can happen to a network is an America that does its own thing.

The Americans have to do their own thing

Verena S. is the national manager of one of the larger medium-sized Western European companies in North America. She runs her business well and turns a good profit. Her management board has one serious problem with her, however. It is not easy to harmonize North American operations with the rest of the world in order to realize the planned synergy effects. »Verena just has to be different!«, the executives say. No form of disciplinary action works with her, not even if it comes straight from the top. Once every three months, the eight national managers meet at European headquarters to find a consensus on issues they have in common. Scarcely have they all returned to their respective countries when the Americans once again do their own thing.

Network leadership is a personal issue.

In spite of this – or precisely because of it – the corporation cannot afford at this time to do without the synergy income, which after all amounts to tens of millions. The head of personnel suggests getting an executive coach with network experience to come in and diffuse the situation. Things get tense, because now the gaping chasm between normal practice and Best Practice starts to widen. Some members of the committee say, »What's that supposed to accomplish? We aren't going to send in a nanny to chase around after our national managers. They should be able to do their jobs on their own. It's what we pay them for!« Proponents of Best Practice won't be taken in by this mistaken way of thinking, however, because they know, »It's a people's business!« – which means: Network leadership is a personal issue rather than an organizational issue.

The company's head of human resources puts it like this, »Just because some old codgers on the management board have something against coaching or against Verena, they are ready to give up almost twelve million in synergy income.« He is absolutely determined to integrate Best Practice into his company, so he works on his executive colleagues until they finally give him the go-ahead. Now it gets down to the nitty-gritty. How will the coach manage to get America back on track?

The selected coach talks with some of the executives and then to Verena and her leading employees. Since no neutral third party has ever done this before, he discovers something that no one has ever found out before: The assignments of blame which are making the rounds are unfounded. Verena has no lack of competency, as some board members have been saying. And the US market is not as different as Verena always claims when trying to push her special wishes through. No, the source of the conflict lies – have you guessed it by now? – in the American mindset. Americans are pioneers. They lead; they do not follow. If, for example, someone suggests that the network pilots take part in a ›fitness program‹ and seven of the country managers approve it, then for that very reason, the Americans won't give it their approval. They do not follow along behind; they lead the way. And if they are not allowed to do so, they will refuse to work together at all and stand defiantly in the corner.

Coaching solves network problems.

By using his keen powers of perception, the coach uncovered not only the reasons for these conflicts, but at the same time a particularly cunning plan for resolving them. If Mohammed won't come to the mountain, then the mountain must come to Mohammed. If seven countries cannot integrate the eighth, then the eighth must integrate the seven. The management board, gathered together to hear the new plan, looked sceptical. »What is that supposed to accomplish?« But the country managers were thrilled. »We'll turn the tables on them! Now the Americans will have to court us and win us over to *their* concepts!« And best of all, the Americans love it! After all, it corresponds to how they view themselves – the leaders of the free world!

A crisis coach is a last resort.

If you are now waving your raised hand because you do not like the idea of making the control of your networks dependent upon external elements, this next topic is for you: A crisis coach is a last resort. It is better to coach managers in such a way that they won't ever need a crisis coach.

Try subject-specific coaching, for example.

Subject-specific coaching

The world is a crazy place. All managers complain about how out of touch and over-theoretical the school systems are. And then the same managers go off and book this type of training for their people! Let's examine this amusing absurdity as it applies to the biggest obstacle to corporate success in these times of globalization, taking as an example a perfectly ordinary, cross-cultural training seminar.

The IT category manager of a southern German company is presently stuck in just such a seminar. He has to go through it because »our Indians have gone crazy.« His company is having such huge problems with their three Indian IT suppliers that they are already talking about partial in-sourcing. The IT category manager attends training, and what does his CPO say after five weeks? »I cannot believe it. The Indians just don't get it! How many cross-cultural training courses do my people need before they get the capability?«

An informal talk with some of the Indian IT people revealed that they were more or less sabotaging the category manager because he was »a rude and disrespectful Westerner« (which an Indian would never express openly but which was quite clearly implied). An analysis of communications between category management and India showed that the category manager is anything but rude and disrespectful. On the contrary, if a mistake in the software is discovered, he talks about it openly, but without blaming or reproaching anyone. That is precisely what he learned to do in his cross-cultural training; never insult the Indians' feelings of competency or national pride (which are basically one and the same) with disguised accusations! An irritated Indian is like a wild animal just coming off a four-week fast – not welcome at any bridge party.

What the cross-cultural trainer and the category manager he was training obviously didn't recognize, however, is the booby-trap present in every type of training course: Every manager complains that what is learned in a seminar does not necessarily work in real life! And that is exactly the case. The IT category manager learned that he should never tell an Indian what he could tell a German, »Damn it! The two bugs in module 24 are still not fixed!« So he says what he believes to have learned in training, »In module 24, there are two mistakes in the subsection having to do with order execution.« Yet that is precisely what makes the Indian angry, for an Indian would never say something like that. He would say, »Perhaps we should look at module 24 again, particularly at the part dealing with order execution. What do you think?« Then he would make his way slowly towards the issue of the mistakes, beating about the bush until the person he is talking to would realize that there were two bugs to be dealt with. If that is the case, why does the IT category manager not behave like that?

Because it is a completely different way of communicating. For 20 years, he has been speaking ›openly and honestly‹, the typical German way. He cannot speak ›Indian‹ overnight just because he practiced it – along with a lot of other things – in a 20-minute role-play! It's like trying to learn to be a golfer by only acting it out in a role-play.

Cross-cultural competence must be learned through a process of change.

And the best and quickest process to bring about change is coaching. I am sorry if this sounds like an advertisement, but Best Practice isn't concerned with that. They put their money on coaching. What is the problem with normal practice? It is this attitude: »I am not going to let psychotherapists get at my supply chain managers! They have no idea about our field of expertise.« True … and false. The true part is that a subject-specific coach must be competent in the field in question. It would be wrong, however, to finish the discussion of subject-specific coaching with nothing but this argument.

A good subject-specific coach must be competent in both coaching and supply chain management.

That is why the best-earning subject-specific coaches are usually former high-flying managers and network leaders who, on top of having had good training as coaches, have also gathered a lot of coaching experience. This trims the problem of subject-specific coaching down to the usual procurement process: Look for the best, investigate and hire. Best Practice has no problem with that, as the following concrete example will demonstrate.

When purchasing begins to think

The CEO of a plant manufacturer wants to reduce costs. He does not build more than 50 percent of his plant (in the small plant-mass production), but has it built or delivered by system suppliers, so he tells his head of purchasing to reduce the costs of the supply chain. The head of purchasing starts a dozen cost reduction projects for the optimization of certain internal processes and a wide range of other measures including the creation and implementation of a category management strategy. All in all, completely normal, sensible and necessary projects for enlightened, modern network management. What happens normally if such absolutely necessary projects get started up?

You guessed it, someone opposes them. Because the rest of the company is not used to purchasing having a mind of its own and making proposals. When people who up until now were labeled as the form fillers suddenly start suggesting groundbreaking projects ... that awakens a lot of ill will and these sensible, necessary projects will be fought against with incredible determination and strength (by some, not by all). It is what Marx commented on the inherent instability of systems: Capitalism would function – if everyone behaved sensibly. But they don't.

In Normal Practice, purchasing tries to start their projects in spite of the unreasonableness of those less mature – and runs into opposition. The head of purchasing of the plant manufacturer had been afraid of that. He had wanted to avoid his project managers having to break their backs fighting against such internal opposition from the beginning. »Anyone who is a project manager in purchasing has to be able to do more than just run projects. He or she has to be able to get experts in the boat. If they don't have this ability, then all of their huge specific competence is of little use.« That is why he engaged a team of subject specific coaches. They figured out the situation relatively quickly.

Sell yourself!

Anyone wanting to carry out successful projects in purchasing has to be fit in self-marketing.

One of the hired coaches described the situation as follows: »The project managers in purchasing were as competent in their area as anyone could hope. However, expert knowledge is not enough to sell a project to stakeholders or business partners.« Instead the opposite is true: They are more likely to turn stakeholders against purchasing and their »incomprehensible and time wasting projects«. Because what is expert knowledge for a purchaser is Greek to the stakeholder. Quite simply because the purchaser does not understand the person he is selling his project to. The Stakeholder does not speak ›purchasing‹.

This normative displays its entire amusing absurdity when you place it in the context of globalized networks. For example, in the context of those supply chains that broke down not too long ago: automobiles, tools, mechanical engineering ... If in such a crisis situation purchasing pops up with the life-saving project, what happens then? Will the project manager be hailed as the Messiah? Not at all.

Not because his project cannot save the network. It can. It is because the specialized departments do not (cannot) understand the Messiah. The plant manufacturer did not want to come close to this tragedy at all, which is why the project managers had to learn to sell their projects first. And themselves. Through subject specific coaching.

Total interdependency

Best Practice would connect everything.

It is unusual for a company to introduce subject-specific coaching as an instrument of change management. Even more unusual was the plant manufacturer's timeline: Subject-specific coaching ran over one year's time. The project managers went into the coaching as group managers, were kitted out with the complementary skills of self-marketing, and were then accompanied through their project work – once to three times a week, equally unusual – and were able at the end to take their projects with them into the company's normal organization as head of their organizational units. And they were also coached in this critical cross-over: That is typical: Best Practice would connect everything.

Put inversely: You cannot connect what is already connected. Best Practice knows these connections. That is very unusual. Many of our coaches were called into problem situations in which an impatient board demanded: »Get project X off the ground! That has to go faster!« It is a very understandable request. But this demand ignores the critical connections: If a project has a stoppage, it is not because of the project. It is of little use to pump up the project managers with project management skills and then help them push their work projects forward more quickly. When the next project comes, we will have the same situation – which makes a lot of consultants really happy. Because it presents them with a never ending flow of new contracts. All because things were separated which are interdependent and belong together. Best Practice takes into consideration these interdependencies from the beginning.

It puts together what belongs together at its core: Pushing the planned projects through quickly and successfully while at the same time making the project manager fitter in communication and marketing, executing the necessary change management in the interfaces of the specialized departments, and carrying out leadership development for the project managers so that they can take over the leadership function afterwards. It sounds a lot like the squaring of the circle.

What's abnormal is to extract single components from this inseparable circle of topics which are connected together and then wanting to ›heal‹ the symptoms with isolated therapies such as training, subject-specific coaching and other special leadership efforts. That does not work. But you have to recognize it first.

At this point I normally have to calm down some board members. Because at this point the usual objection emerges: »An entire year? Three times a week? Coaching? We don't have so much money. And definitely not now!« Let me tell you a little secret: No one has the money. Not even Best Practice. But still they coach. Do they have the Midas touch?

The Midas touch of Best Practice: Value, not cost

Of course, such a one-year coaching supplement costs a lot of money – do not believe anyone trying to convince you otherwise. Developing good coaching concepts and paying the coaches has to be done up-front.

Best Practice does not calculate up-front. It calculates based on the bottom line, and coaching based on the bottom line is not an expense but a profit. The plant manufacturer's purchasing manager said: »Coached projects go much faster, with less friction and more synergy. That ensures a return for the coaching costs.« But that is not all.

Best Practice managers calculate with value, not with expenses.

Coached projects also create so many cost reductions and potential efficiency increases during their development (which normally fall by the wayside during the usually hectic days of a project) that they not only finance themselves, but would show a favorable profit, if only financial supply chain management were capable of showing these end-of-year contributions in the P&L made by Purchasing. But this is actually unnecessary. A good purchasing manager does not need a P&L statement to see that coached projects have made a clear return on the investment. This means: Best Practice managers calculate with value, not with expenses.

Although every manager claims that it is only important »what the bottom line shows«, amazingly, only Best Practice managers convert this trivial slogan into reality. They draw the line where others only see the costs. It becomes clear within this context how risky it is to omit the popular saying: »We don't have money for that!« Even if it was true (which generally is not the case), it exposes the manager as a cost thinker, not as a value thinker. I would be reluctant to be caught on the street with this label, because any housewife knows that it does not matter how much the oranges for the child cost, as long as the return is positive: If the child is diagnosed with a vitamin deficiency at some point, the vitamins are more expensive.

Because Best Practice managers think differently, they can act differently.

Because Best Practice managers think differently they can act differently. Different thinking is especially reflected in such abstract structures as the value of an investment. But it can be even more abstract: Let's talk about communications.

Talking like Cicero

Communications make up 90 percent of management. Almost everyone knows this, but it is only implemented in Best Practice. This can be clearly seen on the example of communications in change management.

In change projects communications are more important than the content of the change.

A Spanish company recently involuntarily conducted a slightly unethical field experiment in the split-run mode: Because of a crisis, it had to terminate 120 employees. 80 of these employees received their termination after an initial meeting with the personnel manager, as is customary; 40 employees were notified by a personnel officer, who communicated great understanding, taking the terminated employees verbally into his arms (real managers would shudder), pulled them out of the role of the victim in a short-term intervention and activated their resources. Unfortunately, one of the country's universities was studying the socio-psychological effects of terminations based on precisely these 120 employees. The result was striking.

Although all of the terminated employees remained in the company for several weeks after receiving the termination (which is logical due to the standard termination notice period), the 80 terminated employees didn't actually do any real work. They didn't look for a new job or alternatives. They were depressed. They were paralyzed with shock. All of the other 40 looked around for alternatives on the job market or in their own company. The moral of the story: The content is unimportant (the termination was the same for all employees). Only the communication of the content is important.

As one of the researchers involved unconventionally put it: »Terminations do not depress people, it is how the termination is communicated.« The natural analogy follows: Purchasing projects do not irritate specialized departments, it is how the purchasing projects are communicated.

Anyone who has attempted to optimize the global network in his company even by one tiny detail knows this. Everyone thinks this is good. Everyone agrees. Everyone promises support, but one area ruler and another opinion leader and yet another official there quietly and secretly bring the project to a halt. Not because they are opposed but because they didn't understand it. »Then the project manager tries to convince the obstructionists of the necessity of teamwork«, management boards say to me. That does not work.

These people have a project, but literally no concept. Normal Practice remains in this concept vacuum in which their projects literally choke. However, every Best Practice manager knows: »No communication without a concept.« An experienced purchasing manager will instruct his coaches to equip the coachees with communication concepts so persuasive and attractive that any internal interface can be detected effortlessly, including ensuring acceptance and active support over the long term for the purchasing projects. This is precisely what the coaches did with their coachees at the above mentioned plant manufacturer.

Managers are no born communicators.

This mistake is two-fold: First, it is assumed that managers can communicate naturally in this way, that they can achieve the desired communication goals quickly without friction, amicably and especially over the long term.

The second mistake is the presumption that it is sufficient to be able to talk in order to sell projects or even standard everyday network tasks within the company. If this was true, our economy would collapse tomorrow because all advertising agencies would close immediately and all marketing teaching positions would be closed. Neither marketing nor advertising would be necessary if it was enough to simply talk to people. But it isn't. It was never like this. This could not save a marriage or sell products or projects.

Anyone that wants to communicate needs a plan, a concept which selects the communication instruments and the argumentation that promises the best success for a particular communication situation, based on the specific motivation of the target group. Which may be understandable; however, the question is: Why do you need a coach for that?

Keeping a sense of proportion

Successful communication is a matter for leaders.

It may seem obvious to demand that a master of the network has enough qualifications to create a communication concept. »After all, he is being paid for it!« CPO's have a different opinion: »It is either unbelievably naïve or downright offensive to expect a project manager to create a communication concept. After all, this is not included in the usual scope of responsibilities for chemists, physicists or engineers!« They basically cannot do that, because they have never learned it. In addition: Successful communication is not a matter for managers, but for leaders.

Managers manage and organize (nothing against that). Leaders lead, because they can communicate in a manner that every departmental ruler will follow immediately and enthusiastically. We have been talking of nothing else for the past 100 pages: We need more leaders! People who can inspire other people so much that they support the necessary projects.

It would be fantastic if project managers could create communication concepts. But if they are only able to do that with the aid of coaches even in Best Practice, this should give informed and interested observers food for thought.

Final question: What is the entire effort worth?

The bottom line

The success of network projects depends very much on the communication of the projects.

Our plant manufacturer's projects are all successfully implemented; the newly introduced processes have all been accepted by the employees and are also being applied. The desired improvements have been achieved and some change processes are still underway.

The satisfaction of the internal business partners has clearly been increased. Not only because the network is functioning more effectively and efficiently but because communications are more effective and efficient.

These communications manage the expectations of the people involved. If the divisional manager thinks that only nonsense will come of a network project, it won't matter if you reinvent penicillin – to him, it will still be nonsense. However, if project communication is successful in convincing the person into being an active participant, he will not only get involved to ensure that the project will be objectively (more) successful. He will also subsequently fully back the resulting successes and issue the network pilot and his department with a good report. And not only that!

The plant manufacturer's purchasing manager admits to an unexpected, but desired side effect of excellent project communications: »The internal business partners have not only understood the project itself thanks to intense communication. They now generally understand our purchasing business and supply chain management much better.«

Communication produces transparency.

This transparency is important for purchasing if they want to be able to design their networks so that not every little economic world crisis can weaken them and if they want to contribute strategically to the company's success with their network management – which is the reason why supply chain management was created.

At a glance: The way to success

- These days coaching is considered to be the most effective and fastest way to success – if the coach has process, leadership, and expert knowledge capabilities.
- Tip: Do not underestimate the number of network problems which can be traced back to the character of whoever is in charge. Coaching helps not only the manager but also the network.
- Tip: Crisis coaching is good. Expert coaching is better. It averts crises.
- Most network problems are not triggered by the network but are in fact communication challenges. Coaching can be especially effective here.
- Tip: Communication is good. A communication concept tailored for internal customers is better.

8 Tomorrow's winners

»Anyone who bought shares in Apple 30 years ago is now a millionaire. If you want to be one of tomorrow's winners, you must do the right thing today.«
James Mills, Supply Chain Manager

The Love Lab

When are you going to be divorced? Will your current relationship outlast the next three years? 99 out of 100 people will answer this question with, »Who knows?« The hundredth person will say, »Ask John Gottman.«

After long years of exacting labor, the University of Washington researcher has empirically established a procedure by which the success of relationships can be predicted with a high degree of accuracy. When a couple enters his institute, which researchers jokingly call »The Love Lab«, he can actually predict with 99 percent precision whether the pair's relationship will outlast the next five years. Amazing? Not really:

Some people are able to recognize today what will fail tomorrow.

This ›gift‹ turned some of them into millionaires, like those who realized 30 years ago that Apple would be ›The Next Big Thing‹.

The most trivial of all secrets of success: If you invest in upcoming trends today you will be rewarded with success tomorrow. It is not only about choosing the right partner or buying the right stocks; it also applies to being successful in global networks. The question is: What should we invest in today so our pockets will be filled with gold tomorrow? Or, to put it another way, what's ›The Next Big Thing‹?

The Next Big Thing

Under no circumstances is it what the masses are doing. The masses didn't buy Apple shares 30 years ago; only those who had a knack for ›The Next Big Thing‹ did. It is still the same today.

What are the masses currently doing? Among other things, they are fervently trying to bring their network managers up to speed in contract law and negotiation leadership because it has become evident that many managers and employees are overtaxed by negotiations and contracts at the international level. Such measures are absolutely necessary. Unfortunately, ›That Which Must Be Done‹ is never ›The Next Big Thing‹. ›That Which Must Be Done‹ is yesterday's news – the exact opposite of ›The Next Big Thing‹.

If Best Practice managers are always one step ahead, then take that step!

Some conclude from this that they can never catch up to Best Practice, because they will always be one step ahead. That is the thinking of a victim; winners think differently: If Best Practice managers are always one step ahead, then take that step!

For once, put today's necessities aside and focus on what will put you ahead tomorrow. For companies, managers and networks, there are essentially three ›Next Big Things‹:

- self-coaching
- crisis management
- change leadership

Self-coaching

What makes someone a manager? What distinguishes him from other managers? His performance capabilities: What can he do? How much can he achieve? Can he keep his cool under fire? Executive coaching is experiencing a boom because especially in these times of crisis, managers are recognizing how quickly and extremely coaching raises their performance capability (if the coach is good. If not – what's the use of having good purchasers?). Unfortunately, the fact that there is a boom in coaching means that even the masses have now discovered it, which is precisely why it is not ›The Next Big Thing‹. Best Practice managers are once again that famous one step ahead.

Best Practice managers use both coaching and self-coaching.

As useful as a (good!) coach can be, he cannot always be there when you need him. Usually, he is unavailable precisely when you need him most. David Foster also found this to be true. He is the head of purchasing at a mid-sized Swiss company. Twice a year, he has to negotiate with a large supplier who, because of the size difference between the two companies, can practically dictate the conditions to him. In the past, this never failed to make him see red. »These power plays! This open intention to exploit us! They think they can treat us as they damn well please!« In the face of such provocation, David used to fly off the handle regularly … and play right into the hands of his adversary. He who loses his cool will lose the negotiation.

At some point David asked me to coach him, to help him prepare himself for these critical meetings. Together we developed a more decisive negotiating strategy, more convincing arguments, and a faster way to handle objections. Afterwards, David really was able to perform better (as was to be expected). Nevertheless, he knew as well as I, »As long as I continue to let that guy provoke me during our conversations, and as long as I have to battle with my emotions, I will never be able to achieve optimum results.« Managers need someone to prepare them, cover their backs and build up their competency and authority before and after going into battle. A coach can provide that. But they also need support *during* the fight (a coach in their pocket, so to say) when the remaining 20 percent of their performance reserves have to be mobilized to make the decisive breakthrough that promises a crowning success. Such a ›pocket coach‹ does exist in the form of self-coaching techniques.

In David Foster's case, there were three disassociation techniques that I showed him during our coaching sessions. He needed to learn to coach himself during critical phases of the negotiations precisely when necessary.

Disassociation techniques are the tools of the world's best poker players, allowing them to see through every bluff and turn it to their own advantage. Disassociation brought David tremendous success. At the next meeting his opponent realized to his amazement that not only did his provocations in effect bounce right off of David, but David was able to turn the tables on him and smile coolly as he backed him into a corner. The adversary lost his nerve for a few minutes and during that time, David wrangled two percent off of the purchase price, a savings that amounted to a five-figure sum. This result is not surprising: Success depends upon experience, competency, and intellect, but even an IQ of 150 is useless if you lose your nerve.

Best Practice managers know this. That is why they arm themselves with self-coaching techniques which are useful not only in guarding against provocation but also in mobilizing aspects of performance potential which are usually beyond a manager's reach. And what is the competition doing? They are still training up on their negotiating techniques. That is the right thing to do, a good thing to do. It is necessary; you really should do it, too. But if it is the only thing you are doing, you are going to overlook ›The Next Big Thing‹.

Crisis management

All sorts of crises, but hardly any crisis management.

Need I say more? Unfortunately, yes, because: We have all sorts of crises, but hardly any crisis management.

If a crisis becomes acute, most people react with astonishment. Mass lethargy, an insistence upon long-outmoded strategies, a hectic and excessive desire for action, curtailing investments, freezing budgets for publicity and training, policies initiating temporary work and dismissals – these are crisis reactions, not crisis management. Best Practice handles things differently.

The crisis reflex of the Best Practice: »Improve your potential!«

Best Practice does its very best to avoid budget freezes and dismissals, making an extra effort during negotiations with banks and unions so they can push through as many investments as possible, go forward with research, and continue to give employees the chance to develop to the best of their abilities. And there is yet another difference: In normal practice, the crisis reflex says, »Bury yourself!« The Best Practice reflex says, »Improve your potential!«

Both are digging, in a manner of speaking, but Best Practice uses its excavations to bring something productive to light. As an example, there was a machine-building company which, like many other machine builders, was stuck in a hopeless situation during the next-to-last crisis at the beginning of the new millennium and didn't have the means to sit out the crisis. Their customers simply weren't buying any new machines. »They are just continuing to work with their old stuff!« the sales engineers complained.

The board of directors could have announced staff cut-backs, but instead they chose crisis management. They established so-called ›potential groups‹ – above all in sales – which had to sniff out latent potential and prepare to make the most of it. One of these groups discovered that although the customers were not buying new machines anymore, their old machines were set up in quite inefficient ways. The flow of goods took too long and was too complicated, the time from the receipt of an order till its dispatch was too long, and the error rate was too high. So the company began to offer consultation in the areas of plant and procedure optimization.

In contrast to some of its competitors, it survived; and what's more, when the worldwide economic crisis broke out eight years later, it showed the smallest decrease in turnover within the entire market sector. Why? Because in the meantime, it was making half of its turnover through consulting.

Crisis competency is a matter of knowing how to exploit your potential.

If this is all so easy, why isn't everyone doing it? Because the very existence of these unidentified capabilities is the best proof that up to now a company hasn't been able to fully exploit its potential. It requires special talent not to be totally shaken by each new crisis that arises, to draw upon previously unexplored potential and come out on top, gaining strength from the crisis and exploiting the chances it has to offer. Best Practice incorporates all of these abilities.

While many others are busy fighting against crises, Best Practice concentrates on achieving crisis competency.

As Marx once said, there is always another crisis just around the corner. Steffen Kröhnert, social scientist at the Institut für Bevölkerung und Entwicklung (The Institute for Population and Development) in Berlin, says, »During my school days in what was then East Germany they taught us that capitalism is marked by cyclical crises. It is true.«

Change leadership

The world has a problem with change; it cannot cope with it fast enough, well enough or for a long enough time. Why? As an example, let's take a look at your average head of purchasing. Many of them – the good ones – should actually be CPOs already. They mention this to the board of directors periodically ... and? Does anything happen? Not a chance! Why not?

The appointment of a CPO is not a question of communication; it is a hierarchical process of change and as such, an issue of change management. What applies to the individual careers of many heads of sales also applies to their networks:

It is a tragedy of our time that the huge challenges of globalization, networks and modern marriage cannot be conquered by communication alone.

The tragedy lies not in the circumstances themselves, but in the fact that they go largely unrecognized ... except in Best Practice, of course.

If you want change, you need change management.

Take the metal working company with locations in ten countries, all still using independent purchasing to cover their enormous energy needs. In this age of globalization! The central head of procurement complains that, »Country A will purchase energy, for example, during certain peak times, for twice the price that country B will. And it is not as if the local energy market is that expensive! It is just that they are poor purchasers!« For years, this head of procurement has recommended organizing centralized category management, an idea which could easily save millions per year. But he cannot push it through. The head honchos in those lands and categories defend what's theirs. Because they are bad people? No. Because the head of purchasing is running things on the basis of communication instead of using the principle of change leadership.

Luckily, at some point this procurement head goes over to the competition. His successor is not only a head of procurement; he is also a change agent. He travels to the ten countries in question, invites the national bosses out for a beer, listens to their worries, asks for their ideas in reference to category management and gets a respected university to draw up an internal ranking for purchasing in the different countries, with particular attention to the category of energy. Then he gets the management board to assign him a project leader with the ability to get things done and who can bring the necessary hierarchical emphasis to the project and force any local honchos who step out of line to shape up. This is change management at its best.

Three months later, he gets the go-ahead for category management, something his predecessor couldn't accomplish in three years. He was an excellent head of purchasing, but his successor is a change leader. And that is why he succeeded in making the change.

Best Practice: Lanxess

Lanxess is a global player with strong roots in Germany that go back as far as 1863, the year Bayer was founded. At the beginning of 2005, during the course of a reorganization at Bayer, portions of its chemical and plastics activities were disincorporated and turned over to the newly founded Lanxess Group, thus combining tradition and long years of experience with the dynamism of a young company.

Lanxess concentrates on premium products throughout the range of its extensive portfolio. Development, production, and sales of high-tech plastics, high-performance rubbers, special chemicals, and intermediate products are the core of its business, which has 14,600 employees at 44 production sites in 23 countries worldwide.

Very few consumers will actually hold these products in their hands, however, because Lanxess produces for producers. Its products flow into other products. For example, the company provides flame retardants for wood used in the construction industry and chemicals for tanning and finishing leather used to produce shoes and furniture. If your chic leather shoes keep your feet dry in the rain, then it is Lanxess. The easiest way for any consumer interested in getting a feel for what the company is about is to hit the print button on his or her computer: Lanxess recently developed a new iron oxide used to produce chemical toner for the latest generation of printers.

Lanxess has a Best Practice nature because although the company battles the usual supply chain problems, it masters them with unusual success. This is no trivial characterization: The network amateur gladly and implicitly assumes that Best Practice only concerns itself with the ›best‹ problems – the ones that have, so to speak, a golden lining. It is a logical mistake, but if top companies only worried about luxury problems they could not be role models for others. So let's have a look at how it all began at Lanxess, which is similar to what you would encounter at any company these days.

Even angels have to start somewhere

The change processes at Lanxess began with what is generally called »blunt analysis«. Even that is fairly unusual.

Best Practice engages in blunt analysis. Others tend to go easy on themselves.

Why? Because blunt analysis hurts. It is just the opposite of the endless lamentations of those who wallow in their martyrdom. If you analyse yourself mercilessly you will discover your own weaknesses. The marked advantage of Best Practice managers is that they have enough inner strength and career stability to enable them to confront their weaknesses – and eliminate them.

The outcome of the analysis was what you experience in almost every company today: too few well-defined, uniform and efficient processes in supply chain management, high material costs, too little transparency internally and in regard to internal customers, too few effective methods of application. In addition, a survey of business partners in several companies showed an urgent desire for more transparency and more customer-oriented purchasing and network control. Above all, internal customers wished that procurement would more fully explain the sense, purpose and advantages behind an action. I believe this wish is shared by every division in every field in every land in the world. It is a wish for this day and age.

What sets Lanxess apart is that those responsible for purchasing have strategically refused to get bogged down in current demands. Holger Hüppler, Head of Purchasing at Lanxess, wanted to fulfill both present and future demands, so he and his team formulated three lines of attack:

- Develop a high rate of change not only for current, but also and above all for future change projects.
- With strongly motivated employees, achieve quick wins, the first after only three months. Implement all newly developed processes within six months.
- Accomplish everything by means of comprehensive restructuring.

To a certain extent, this triad of goals represents a refusal of »Kaizen«, the Japanese philosophy of continuous change. Continuous is out. Continuous is too slow in these extremely fast times of globalization.

These days, it is speed of change that counts.

One should be able to change at least as fast as the market and environment, or even faster, if possible. One? Well, actually it is only the movable parts of a company that can change – people. That is why Lanxess put together a fitness program designed to bring managers and employees up to speed.

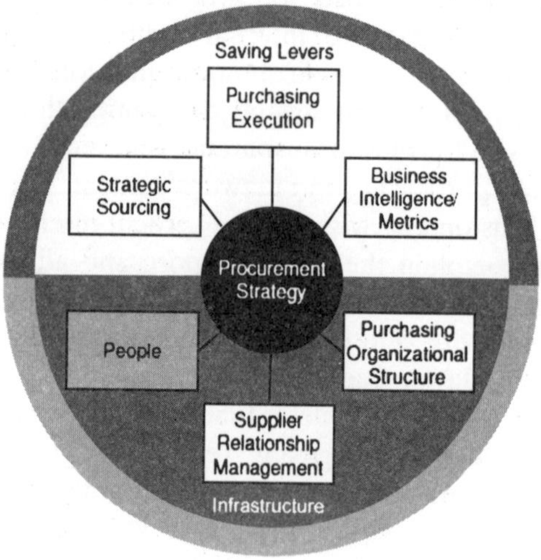

Source: Lanxess AG

Figure 13: Lanxess Wheel of Excellence in Procurement

The fitness program

Up until ten years ago, the prevailing opinion recommended that anyone who wanted to lose weight should go on a diet. It actually should have been evident long before – if it were only that easy! – that dieting alone does not do the trick. That is not only true for dieting:

A combination program works a lot better than any one measure on its own.

Anyone who only goes on a diet has a fairly poor chance of achieving lasting weight loss. If, however, that same person regularly trains to build stamina, does a bit of power training, changes his or her daily exercise habits and, above all, eating habits over the long-term, he or she can almost be guaranteed a lasting weight loss. The program makes the difference. The Lanxess program consists of:

- An assessment center for internal and external candidates, in order to fill the new positions that were necessitated by the restructuring.
- The introduction of job rotation for network drivers and purchasers – one of the best methods for providing employees with the standing necessary for being accepted by the specialized departments.

Purchasers who have been around and seen more than just their same old desk in the procurement department are more competent, have a better sense of the business and a better understanding of the interdepartmental supply chain and, in addition, enjoy a better standing in the specialized departments.

- A classic training program which no allround fitness program should lack, covering everything from supplier management to risk management, from negotiations training to self-marketing, and rounded out by coaching measures.
- The planning of a special training program for top performers: the pipeline for high potentials. This is to be recommended in general, since the promotion of the highly talented should be separate from the fitness program for the rank and file.
- Lanxess introduced an incentive system. Why so?

An incentive system for purchasing? That is typical Best Practice. The idea is so obvious that up to now it has been mostly ignored. In many companies, sellers are provided with so many bonuses, prizes and incentives that you might think you are at a raffle instead of in a sales division. At the same time, purchasers who save the company millions are expected to be content with their salaries alone. This is not only illogical and unfair, but also uneconomical and not very cost-conscious, because even in supply chain management, the following holds true:

What will be rewarded will be done.

A purchaser with incentives is a much more successful purchaser. As I said, the subject is not new. All those responsible for purchasing talk about it, but apparently only Best Practice converts talk into action. At Lanxess, supply chain management now has an incentive program with observable success: Those who are rewarded perform better.

The principles

Principles provide orientation and allow you to act with confidence. They are the guiding light for all larger developmental projects. Conditions change so quickly these days. Today, corporate procurement universities are all the rage ... but what about tomorrow?

Principles stay the same.

They give orientation, support and motivation and more often than not they set into motion the further development of structures and processes.

1. Network development is people development!

What a great motto to help lead the way out of a deplorable state of affairs! Companies all over the world now know very well how to develop machines and facilities. In the development of intangible constructions like networks or even people, however, large sectors of the business world are still Neanderthals.

If you write in-house memos instead of training your employees, you are using hindsight.

Not at Lanxess. Here they realize that networks cannot be improved upon very much through managerial decisions or by hiring new network leaders or making other structural changes. It is much more effective to train the people who operate these networks. A lot of managers have a really hard time coming to this realization. Recently, I read yet another in-house memo in which a production manager exhorted workers to more fully examine parts being supplied by Asia. Inspecting components upon arrival is too late. What is needed is on-site inspection. But his network managers simply didn't have the market savvy to assign the task to a competent local purchasing organization. Ergo: If you write in-house memos instead of training your employees, you are using hindsight.

2. Separate operative and strategic procurement!

With strategic purchasing, Lanxess focuses on bundling volumes, benchmarking and negotiation. With operative purchasing, the focus is on processing and demand management. As a reminder: These must be separated structurally and organizationally! A purchaser cannot rush through 500 orders per day while at the same time quasi incidentally negotiating strategic partnerships. One or the other will suffer (usually the other – the strategic procurement). Only a separation of the two activities will lead to the desired success.

3. Orientation of procurement should be two-dimensional.

At Lanxess they have global category managers on the one hand responsible for their individual product groups worldwide and business unit procurement managers on the other who work on specific subjects relating to the company's business partners. This matrix organization of the networks may not be the perfect solution, but it is still the most practical procedure because it is relatively easy to understand and implement.

4. Implement processes for agreeing on goals!

People love to complain about the silent war between the specialized departments and procurement. They cannot ever agree. They have different goals. These are actually no grounds for conflict, just perfectly normal differences in interests. The problem is not that the specialized departments and procurement have divergent interests – married couples usually have them, too. He wants to watch a sportscast while she wants to talk about their relationship. This only becomes a problem when these diverging interests are not managed. For precisely this reason, Lanxess cultivates a suitable goal-agreement process.

5. Set up a global procurement committee.

This should be made up of selected business unit leaders. It is not enough to simply talk about intentions for how to control the network: You also need to set up suitable structures. Suitable means that if once again only network managers are sitting on such a committee, network control will continue to face the well-known problems of interfacing with the business units. Network guidance concerns everyone. Therefore, all area heads should be represented on such a guidance committee. If this seems impossible to push through in your company, it is easy to pinpoint the reason: As soon as the board of managers signals its commitment, the whole company will accept and, more importantly, participate in the new interdepartmental structures for network control. No one wants to provoke the board of managers.

6. Tools and databases need to be globalized.

Everyone should really take this principle to heart: We live in the age of globalization. Yet in every land involved in the global networks, different processes, tools, and databases are used. This simply cannot go on. If nobody takes up the cause of necessary standardization, we shouldn't be surprised if it does not happen.

What is really important

Best Practice at Lanxess, which you have just read about, began by having some managers, purchasing heads and CPOs evaluated. Everyone was naturally impressed, no question about it. But one of the testers then added, »What impressed me most were not the successes of Lanxess. They are naturally indisputable. But I have to ask myself: That was a huge expenditure of time, energy and money. How did they do it? Was it in addition to their normal work? Aren't they drowning in operational hectic like the rest of us?« In a relaxed tone of voice, someone then uttered a great truth:

Best Practice managers can free themselves from the dictates of urgency.

Theoretically, the inversion of this argument constitutes a paradox: Because Best Practice already has leaders who can tell the difference between what is urgent and what is necessary, it gets more leaders for its networks. Those who do not have these capable leaders also cannot get any! But as stated, this is only a paradox when viewed theoretically.

Recently, a CPO whose network control had just confronted this paradox came up with a practical solution. He said, »If this is true, then I will simply free up five of my best operative purchasers. From now on, they are to concern themselves with strategics alone.« So. That is that. A good practitioner does not allow paradoxes to get in his way.

At a glance: The Next Big Thing

- Tip: Adopt today what will be crucial tomorrow.
- Especially: self-coaching, crisis management, change leadership.
- The manager of tomorrow takes advantage of coaching and can coach himself.
- The manager of tomorrow does not suffer from the ever-growing number of crises: He manages them.
- The manager of tomorrow stands at the forefront of change. He does not regard it as simply a factor of the environment, but as his personal challenge and responsibility. In addition, he has not only mastered his instruments for change, he actually uses them.

9 My own university!

»If a trainee does not know how to do a rule of three equation, some of our master mechanics will complain about how rotten the school system is. The others will teach him how to do it.«
Stefan Knauss, Trainer in Mechanical Engineering

Corporate Procurement University

If you want to understand world economics you have to go to the cinema. Thriller? Comedy? Erotic? Action? Actually, it does not really matter what kind of film you see. All that matters is that you don't (God forbid) watch a DVD instead … and that the audio portion of the movie cuts out. This is what happened to me a few weeks ago.

First the jokers made themselves known: »Wow, it's loud in here!« Then came the grumblers. One of them whistled, then several started to curse. Sixty adults sat in a movie theater, watching a film with no sound and swearing like sailors.

At some point, after a full ten minutes, somebody stood up – a man of about 60 or so, middle row, middle seat. He fought his way past the feet of those in his row – who were cursing him every step of the way! – and went into the lobby to tell the projectionist about the problem. The projectionist went back in, turned the sound back on and that was that. Since then, the renowned chairs of some business schools have seriously been considering to require students working on their masters' degrees to take field trips to the cinema (and arrange for the sound to go off ›unexpectedly‹). Nothing could illustrate better the pathetic collective failure of mankind in the face of a capitalistic crisis. And nothing explains more quickly the phenomenon of Best Practice.

Best Practice: 60 people have the same idea ... but only one actually does something about it.

The lack of qualified personnel is one of the biggest challenges in global networks, and it is currently frustrating global cinemas. Cinemagoers gripe about the universities which are not capable of providing enough qualified graduates to fill the vacancies in logistics and supply chain management. (Germany, for example, has a gap of several thousand each year.) And while everyone in the cinema is still complaining away, here and there a few lone souls rise to the challenge under the jealous glares of the passive masses. In this case, by ceasing to complain about universities and founding their own university. It is no joke. In principle, anyone can do it. All you have to do is pluck up your courage, stand up, and go tell the projectionist.

Do not complain about universities! Start your own!

Just imagine it: your own university, for your own networks. And it has got its own name: The Supply Chain University. Its sister school, called the Corporate Procurement University (CPU), is only concerned with developing leaders in purchasing and procurement.

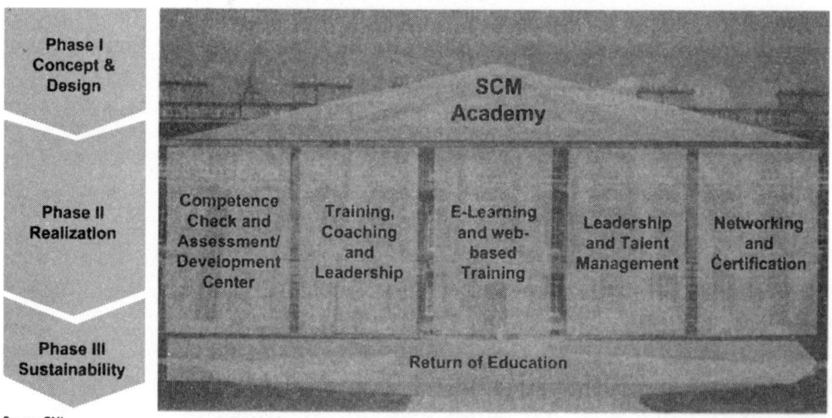

Source: SMI

Figure 14: Supply Chain Academy

To put an end to the cinema metaphor: The phenomenon of cinema-going masses all suddenly jumping up and following the front runner, each now wanting to bring the problem to the projectionist's attention, has never been observed ›in the wild‹. In the wild world of business, however, the CPU movement of Best Practice has started a cult of its own.

Cargo cult management

Shortly after WWII, the Americans maintained a military base on a small Pacific island. The natives, still living in their relatively unspoiled habitat, experienced a kind of spill-over effect (like all neighbors of army bases): The Americans had brought with them not only soldiers and airplanes, but also jobs, exotic foodstuffs, medicines and Coke. When they left, they took all of these comforts and conveniences back with them. Some of the natives felt the loss strongly and thought up ways to remedy the situation.

They had observed that the steel birds with the many wonderful new things landed on long paths flanked by tall towers in which men with strange ear protectors sat and spoke into small buttons suspended in front of their mouths. So, they cleared away strips of forest, built towers out of bamboo and set up straw dolls wearing hemp headsets inside them. They hoped to entice those foreign gods of the yummy chocolate bars to return. In their pursuit of a Snickers bar, they created a cult. That was 60 years ago. This type of remedial strategy has since been known as Cargo cult management.

Modern managers naturally don't do such things any more. They don't start a cult just to get a candy bar. They start one to get their own university. Many top managers are so entranced by the idea of their own university that they rush to put a »Supply Chain University« sign over the door that once led to »Procurement Training«, hoping that this simple bamboo manœuvre would attract the foreign gods of network leadership excellence. It goes without saying that this cult is just as enduringly unsuccessful as the one 60 years ago out in the middle of the Pacific. These days, a Corporate Procurement University (alongside good business schools) is the best place to develop specialists in network leadership, because CPUs are based (among other things) upon two central tenets which, instead of laboring over bamboo, work with the ›real thing‹:

- Integrated coaching
- Integrated change projects

Let's examine both elements of success in a real CPU.

Integrated coaching

The fact that nowadays (almost) every manager with network responsibility wants to start his own university has something to do with the undertow effect of management trends. And above all, it is something this comparison makes a bit clearer: A well-led corporate university is to a normal training program what a Porsche is to a Mini. Both are (good) cars, but to any person wanting to leave the onlookers in the dust, the choice is relatively easy. There's a good reason for that:

Even the most perfectly conceived standard training programs make a learning transfer notoriously difficult.

In standard training programs it is nearly impossible to train network pilots quickly enough to ›fly blind‹. Even participants in good programs can cram until they drop, however, this eagerness to learn does not do them much good when they are back on the job. For decades now, the transfer of training into practice has proven minimal. The reason has also been clear for years: The trainer is never available when he is needed most – when it is time to put the training into practice. Where is he then? He's gone – probably off to the next training session. This concept of training is a transfer-killer which has been known for decades. So how has it been dealt with so far?

Usually with terse verbal brush-offs like, »If you have problems putting your knowledge into practice, just go over the seminar materials again!« In worst case scenarios, the employees remaining unsuccessful for several months were promptly whisked away to attend yet another training session on the same subject. Which did not help either because it was a problem of transfer, not of training. Some companies, and especially certain divisions, have been living in this state of emergency for years: Many sales representatives, for example, are being trained once a year in how to make a sale – without any noticeable transfer. Often the transfer can be negative because the people are so reluctant to go. »Not another ›make the sale‹ training session! What a waste of time!« – which is true because it constitutes a self-fulfilling prophecy.

In extreme cases, if a manager or employee absolutely cannot transfer the training into practice, he will be dispatched to a coach. That will always help (if the coach is good). So why are you still hesitating? Best Practice used to do so, too. A Best Practice manager once admitted to me, »We send our people to training and when they come back they don't put any of it into practice. We sit there impatiently, drumming our fingers on the desk, until we are so frustrated that we send them to a coach as a last resort – and suddenly they're able to implement everything they learned. It makes you kind of wonder: Why do we sit there getting angrier and angrier before we finally call in a coach? Why don't we just call him to begin with?« The CPU recipe for success was born.

Normally, employees are only coached in cases of emergency. At a CPU, they are coached as a matter of routine.

And not (as is usually the case) only when absolutely necessary. Instead, coaching is a habit, natural and immediate, so that the need is never allowed to arise (and cause harm). Everyone trained is automatically coached in precisely what is needed most – putting training into action. That is why comparing a CPU graduate to a graduate of conventional training programs is like comparing a Porsche to a Mini.

Naturally, training that integrates coaching into its program is more expensive than stripped-down ›barebones‹ training! That is why until now, only Best Practice managers have been able to set up genuine corporate universities. And it is not because they have more money. It is because they can do the math.

Who is normally held accountable for employee improvement? Unfortunately, it is the trainer. He hears this managerial dodge every day, »Trainer, make my people better!« And denial is not just a river in Egypt ... the avoidance of responsibility couldn't be more obvious. The manager shoves the responsibility for his employees – supposedly his most valuable asset – onto the hapless trainer. If that really worked, we wouldn't need executives. If that worked, we'd have socialism …

Normal practice is about training. Best Practice is about transfer.

Best Practice managers don't succumb to the temptation of shirking responsibility. They shoulder responsibility for employee improvement. If you delegate this responsibility to others you send your employees to a training program and pray that they will come back ›new and improved‹. But those who take this responsibility on board do everything necessary to ensure that their employees truly improve – even if that means paying for their coaching.

It is a little difference which makes a big difference. It also extends to something that every average seminar attendant hates: projects.

Integrated change projects

People have begun to realize that conventional training has been side-stepping reality for quite some time now. Training programs often tout ›the project‹ as a way back to the real world. After the seminar, each participant has to work on »a project that ideally puts into practice what was learned during training«. That is what the brochure says. The reality looks a bit different.

In reality, participants expend their energy not in implementing a project, but in trying to get out of doing it. Projects are almost never finished because they are not practical and not really useful on the job. There is usually no time set aside to do them and they go against one of the fundamental principles of common sense:

What gets rewarded gets done.

But who rewards the participant and checks on the success of his project? Certainly not his boss. He has too little time for that. So many companies hold follow-up days during which the project's success is supposed to be checked. But even this does not encourage the participant to implement the project if it competes with his daily duties. It does not help him to do his job. In fact, it does just the opposite; it keeps him from doing it. Best Practice managers do not solve this enormous transfer problem by reinventing the wheel. This, by the way, is one of the basic principles of Best Practice:

Best Practice managers also include projects at their company universities, but they are worked on over two ›semesters‹ and discussed during the second semester as well, which is why no one can afford to return from the break without having done his or her project. In addition, the projects at a CPU are completely different from standard projects:

Best Practice managers don't do different things; they just do things differently.

Example	1st year	2nd year
Professional and methodical Skills	• Supplier management • Bestvalue country sourcing • Total cost of ownership • Price structure and cost analysis	• Performance measurement • Process management • Risk management • Analytics and portfolio management
Soft Skills	• Negotiation basics and advanced • Communication & conflict management • Customer orientation	• Confident Leadership • Creating strong teams • Excellence
Business Impact with Project Reports	Identification of new markets and specific categories, and description of integration processes for new suppliers	Checking internal and supplier processes and development of value creation levers and potentials
Coaching	Support in implementing training input into daily business and accompaniment during negotiation processes	Support in implementing training input into daily business

Source: SMI

Figure 15: Exemplary curriculum of a Supply Chain Academy

This distinction is made clear by the experience of a medium-sized business that tried to bring its network pilots up to speed a few years ago. The trainer assigned the following project: »Design a strategy for a new metal product range, including a five-year outlook for supplier development!« Only two out of fourteen trainees even gave it a try. The other twelve said, »What nonsense! We don't have a new metal category. We can't even handle the old supplier!« Two years later, the head of purchasing of that company (now promoted to CPO) founded his own university.

At a CPU, there are no ›learning‹ projects. Instead, there are ›innovation‹ projects.

Now the project assignment (which was almost the same) was titled: »Change the strategy of our light metal category so that it will achieve a cost reduction of 10 percent, while at the same time strengthening innovation!« The three network pilots who chose this project confided to me, »I can't believe it! This is the same project our boss told us he planned to implement anyway! I've been going around in circles trying to find a solution. And now the whole thing is going to be discussed with our trainers, a member of the management board and two professors from the business school after our presentation. In other words, they're going to help us with our annual bonus! Isn't that fantastic?« If this is so great, why are only Best Practice managers doing it?

A tough job

Learning projects cost money. Change projects make money.

There is a reason why many companies commit ›label fraud‹ and stick a »CPU« sign on their procurement training program and then carry on as usual. Conceptualizing projects that have a guarantee of being achieved is back-breaking work. Consider this: When a buyer presents his new category strategy, the trainer must be able to tell him whether it is the right one. To do that, he himself first has to know what the right one is and above all why it is the right one. So he has to do the work of a business consultant before the participants work on their presentations. That requires the appropriate expertise, time, and budget. Outside of Best Practice, the credo is »We have neither the time nor the money!« When Best Practice managers hear that, they often laugh out loud, »We don't have the money either! The project will finance itself!«

A Corporate Procurement University pays for itself.

CPU change projects do not just finance themselves; they actually finance the CPU. That is why badly off companies not only *can* afford their own CPU but *have to* afford it. Assuming the buyers in our example develop a new category strategy for light metal and actually manage to cut costs by 10 percent – then that is a lot of new income compared to which even a substantial CPU trainer fee seems like peanuts. Or to put it more bluntly:

But there is even more. Many change projects produce such a high ROE (Return on Education) that after deducting the CPU costs, there is still a fat profit margin left over at the end of year results. A CPU that functions well is like an elite establishment for cost-saving and efficiency-improving projects which foster innovation.

At a CPU, training goes from being a cost factor to success driver.

In addition to integrated coaching and integrated change projects, the CPU owes its success to a few other factors. Two of them are:

- A CPU is employee development that puts strategy into practice. If a company's strategy is to be an innovation leader, then its CPU won't just teach how to conduct negotiations, but how leaders in innovation should conduct negotiations.
- A CPU does not train ›lock, stock and barrel‹. It is oriented towards specific positions. It does not subscribe to the principle of »Let's train 20 people with high potential and then see what we can use them for.« Instead, as Dr. Norbert Flüggen, Chief Sourcing Officer from Altana says, »In three years, our supply chain will need 20 project leaders who will have to handle 200 projects – and these 20 are precisely the ones we'll train right now.«

As incredibly successful as a well-run CPU can be, it has one crucial disadvantage.

The fly in the ointment

I doubt there is a single board of directors in the entire world that would not like to set up their own university – the sooner the better. Yet, only very few will accomplish this. Why? Because it seems almost impossible to get all the national managers into one boat.

Facts will not sabotage joint efforts as much as fears will.

Their point is always the same: »Central office wants to lump us all together!« This is nonsense, of course. No one who creates a CPU is naïve enough to eliminate country specific variables from their overall equation. What is true for an intercultural marriage is also true for a company university.

If you want to set up a CPU you cannot do so without first initiating change management.

If a country manager even suspects that the company intends to lump his area together with others, his knee-jerk reaction will be to get his veto in as quickly as possible, regardless of whether or not the intention actually exists. If you want to set up a CPU you cannot do so without first initiating change management.

Every CPO who ever successfully founded a CPU first travelled around for six months, seeking the support of the national managers, before ever mentioning those three taboo words. Is that neurotic? No, that is communication.

Once again we see: Management is 90 percent communication. If you can communicate you will be rewarded with a CPU, if you can't you are left with cargo cult management.

A prophet has no honor in his own country

In times of enormous cost pressures it is tempting, of course, to make a cost-intensive project like a CPU somewhat more compatible with the budget. For example, by not hiring ›expensive‹ external trainers and making use of internal trainers instead. For some Best Practice companies like Nestlé or Daimler this proved to be amazingly successful. However, outside of Best Practice such a venture usually gets into difficulties. And for a good reason.

Usually, internal trainers are pelted with eggs and tomatoes, booed, tarred, feathered and chased off the stage – at least in the imaginations of their bored students. Or as HR developers sometimes euphemistically put it: Training programs with internal trainers suffer chronically from acceptance problems.

If you decide to choose trainers from an internal pool you should not choose the ›experts‹.

It is the job of Best Practice to anticipate these problems and take them seriously enough to solve them cleverly. How? The supply manager of a Spanish investment goods manufacturer, for example, said goodbye to these common practices which are the main cause of an acceptance problem right from the start: If you decide to choose trainers from an internal pool you should not choose the ›experts‹.

They generally (there are exceptions) have a huge motivational problem, which is understandable against the backdrop of their dual burden: In addition to their actual work they also have to train! This problem is often accepted as given. Not by the Spanish CPO. He believed: »We are not going to choose trainers who can do everything except for motivating participants to learn.« That makes sense, yet it is in contrast to general practice: In most companies the employees who are especially gifted with expertise and able to find the time to ›somehow fit it in‹ are usually the ones who are supposed to train. A widespread misconception: Lots of football team managers still believe that the best football players are also the best football coaches – although teams around the world impressively prove the opposite every weekend.

Best Practice managers choose only those internal trainers who are popular with most employees.

Those who are liked and admired by everyone. Their words ring true. And they will be accepted as role models and mentors. That is a clever move. This personal acceptance means that the acceptance problem of the training program is automatically solved: Acceptance is a personal matter. It usually fosters the motivation of participants and, of course, the success of the transfer.

Acceptance is often overlooked as a transfer factor.

The usual case is that it really does not matter what participants say about a training program as long as they cram their brains full of stuff. This principle of pounding it in does not work at a CPU because it should above all lead to change, for example, when it comes to the harmonization of cross-border processes.

All countries in one boat

The Spanish company took on the challenge of implementing worldwide uniform purchasing processes and product group strategies. While to the lay person this may sound like a boring administrative task in practice, it is about as boring as a burning stick of dynamite on a birthday cake.

The explosiveness of this task is fuelled by two factors. First of all, the necessary harmonization cannot be prescribed by a ruling. Even if the order for a particular uniform cross-border purchasing process comes ›right from the very top‹ it doesn't mean that the distant buyers, far away from head office, will remember this in the hectic day-to-day business. International subsidiaries of globalized companies are famous for not being very enthusiastic about implementing things that are mandated by head office. Every purchasing manager knows what some of his staff get up, they sometimes ignore SAP processes and, now and again, submit 10,000 dollar orders scribbled on a bit of paper, just like that, with the reasoning that »It used to be OK before!«

Secondly, even with a great deal of goodwill, it won't work. Country-specific implementation of directives usually does not work because of country-specific implementation problems. Moreover, the international subsidiaries themselves do not have the necessary change management skills to overcome these problems.

Current practice grapples with these two challenges by trying it over and over again. The tone of the directives from head office gets increasingly tough until the parent company and the subsidiary are at loggerheads and then some sort of semi-compromise is made – and the supply (chain) manager of the international subsidiary basically carries on doing what he thinks is right.

If you want to achieve something in faraway places you do not send a letter but an ambassador.

The Spanish took a proactive approach to this challenge and nominated, so to speak, harmonization ambassadors, roughly four dozen of them. It is one thing when the far flung head office presents me, as a country manager, a management board directive and expects me to stick to it. It is quite another matter when the far flung head office is suddenly standing in front of me, in the shape of an ambassador, and is able to answer my questions about the management board directive at first hand and to my satisfaction.

Based on this very reason, countries do not have an email account located in foreign countries but an ambassador. Anyone who wants to accomplish something in a foreign country preferably sends an ambassador. This also relates to the old slogan: Think global, act local. The Spaniards sent their ambassadors all over the world – and encountered the same problem in every country.

The same problems in every country

The four dozen ambassadors not only dealt with the work of convincing people and explaining things. They also trained their colleagues in these countries to use standard processes. They encountered the same problem in all of the countries.

Expertise is not the solution.

For example, if a directive from head office specifies that a category position matrix must always be consulted prior to a certain purchasing decision, the CPU ambassador has to be very familiar with matrix. And that is precisely why no one understands it. Each one of us has experienced this effect in the electronics supermarket: The salesman who wants to sell us a TV or HiFi system, a cell phone, a notebook or a personal computer has (ideally) top qualifications. Despite this, no one understands him. Despite this? Because of this! He is using technical jargon.

Globalization is a didactic problem.

In order not to export this phenomenon to other countries of the network, the Spanish ambassadors were trained not only professionally, but also methodically and didactically for one week before being deployed. Even here, Best Practice managers excel: Internal trainers generally receive a crash course over an extended weekend – with nothing but work specific content. Pedagogically and didactically they remain untrained. What is being overlooked: Globalization is primarily a didactic problem.

A true conqueror of the world will obviously be enormously irritated by this: This is about dominance! Control! And at the very least, efficient networks! However, it is not about didactics!

But that is exactly the case. Just consider that many average companies cannot control their networks even by using ambassadors.

Many network ambassadors are in fact double agents, moles, and defectors.

That means that they train the decentralized elements of their global networks based on the central training concept in a way that existing country distinctions are not eliminated, but maximized. They do not train according to the tenets made by the management board but by the country manager. So they just make everything worse!

Every manager with some international experience knows or at least suspects this. However, only Best Practice managers draw the necessary educational and methodological conclusions from that, and they are able to implement it over the long haul.

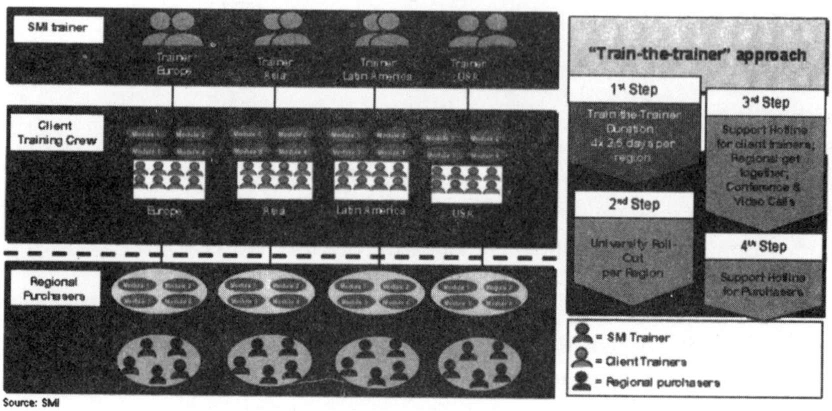

Source: SMI

Figure 16: Train-the-Trainer Approach

The tenacity of Best Practice

The Spaniards gave themselves almost two years from the initial idea to the final training program, not only for the standardization of the purchasing processes, but to advance other topics as well in which the international buyers were trained, for example, advanced sourcing strategies, supplier management & development, supplier risk management, and strategic cost management.

Not only was the CPU concept created during these two years, but the four dozen ambassadors were selected from the countries, trained at corporate headquarters and then sent back to their home countries as ambassadors. Since then, they have been training there. Anyone can translate this exercise into ›enormous costs‹! What are the expenses of two years of training effort? And are these flat-rate costs? Can I influence them? Is the cost-effectiveness eliminated? Of course not! And this is another small distinction which makes a big difference:

Companies spend a lot of money on training and network fitness – and achieve a modest return on education. Best Practice managers also and specifically pursue tough cost efficiency for network development and obtain great results for little money.

The Spaniards are not only Best Practice because their CPUs are very effective but because they are also very efficient. The buyers lived up to their reputations by purchasing the external CPU services with extreme cost-conciousness, by selecting internal, cost-effective trainers right from the start and by always using their red pen during each phase of network activity, continuing to negotiate and renegotiate according to targets.

Global networks cannot be developed without local ambassadors.

Cost efficiency at an operative level is one thing. Another is the strategic cost-benefit calculation. »CPU? Too expensive!« This is one argument from the manual of self-sabotage. If it is not possible to reach this goal differently, faster or for the long term, an internal training system must first be created. The long term effects of such systems convert them from a cost factor into an investment:

This may seem paradoxical: The local ambassador of an international company ought to be the chief of the country or even the local departmental boss! »That,« says the Spanish CPO, »is a popular misconception of globalization.« A Brazilian purchasing manager will train his buyers just as little as a German purchasing manager will. He needs a trainer for this. And this trainer ought to train according to the requirements of corporate headquarters.

Best Practice managers think like athletes: The longer the start-up, the greater the jump.

Where does this tenacity come from? From the ability to think recursively. Actually, the Spaniards ›only‹ wanted the best buyers. In order to achieve their goal they would have to use standard global purchasing processes. Since this project was ›doomed to fail from the beginning‹, the Iberians took a step back and first designed a procurement university. Since this could only be successful with didactically and methodically trained ambassadors, they took a step back and first trained their ambassadors. Since this would only be possible with a sophisticated train-the-trainer program, they took another step back and first designed this program.

Of course, every company wants the best employees, managers, buyers and supply (chain) managers. However, most of them want to jump immediately to get the project going. Only Best Practice managers have the tenacity for an extended start-up – and consequently jump further. This is only fair and reasonable: The one with the longest start-up will be rewarded with the longest jump. The laws of gravity also apply in globalization.

At a glance: Start your own University!

- For years to come the universities will not be churning out enough network managers. The usual corporate skills training measures won't help.
- Tip: Do not complain about the universities. Set up your own: a Supply Chain University (for purchasing, procurement, supply management, logistics and supply chain management) or a Procurement University (for purchasing, procurement and supply management).
- Use all make-or-buy options – from the completely virtual corporate university to the purchase of a concept and trainers.
- Tip: Coaching and change projects are part of the standard curriculum of a corporate university.
- A corporate university can recoup the expenses merely from the benefits of change projects.

10 The executive's best friend

»Change your pleasures, but never your friends.«
Voltaire

The fall of Troy

Who was responsible for the downfall of Troy? Some of you may remember Ulysses from your time at school, that was the Greek with the wooden horse.

History bestowed upon him the title of »The Cunning One« because of his brilliant deceptive manœuvre outside the city of Troy. He is still famous and revered for this decisive strategic ploy that turned the outcome of the battle in favor of the Greeks. Only few know that Ulysses created a strategy for success which several thousand years later still advances generals and management boards from success to success – in its modern application. Ulysses may have led only the final victorious campaign by himself, taking credit for all of the glory until today – the dream of every strategist and general. He was clever enough to make the world believe that this strategy arose from his genius alone, that's why he will remain the greatest general ever for true strategists – while in fact he had a super-brain at work for him in the background quietly and in secret.

We have to thank Homer for the fact that the name of this secret, behind-the-scenes strategist was not overlooked and brought to the attention of the modern world: Nestor, or »Nestor the Wise«, has become a synonym for assured success. A ›nestor‹ is someone with progressive knowledge who has seen everything and always has useful advice at hand. He does not waste time backing the runners-up, instead he unerringly supports the general who will come out ahead in the end and – best of all – lets his general elect have all the glory.

When the frustrated Greek foot soldiers complained impatiently, or army heroes like Achilles sulked and fought against a joint effort, when the field commanders were bickering, or yet another battle strategy went to pieces on the Trojan ramparts, it was always Nestor who came forward with carefully planned diplomatic actions and innovative ideas. He smoothed over troubled waters, spoke words of unification, engineered new strategies – and let his commanding general of the moment reap the benefits of sudden success.

Anyone reading Homer must approach his œuvre with a supremely strategic eye to be able to understand Nestor's role in turning the tides of battle between the famed deeds of Hector, the Lion of Troy, and the heroic exploits of the invincible Achilles. »Nothing has changed since,« comments Thorsten Schiefer, who has been following in Nestor's footsteps for over 15 years and enjoys reading Homer for consolation. He needs consolation because, »When a strategy I have been recommending proves successful, the management board takes all the credit. In the end, of course, this is precisely my goal.«

The Nestors of global network leadership operate in secrecy.

They don't mind doing so without the glory they deserve. The problem is that in contrast to Ulysses, many modern generals miss their cue when it is time to order the deployment of a Nestor.

Missed cues

Despite a huge crisis in sales, an English investment goods manufacturer is doing pretty well. He had been making a comfortably profitable living by successfully combining transmission parts from Kuala Lumpur with designs from New York. His global network ran smoothly and turned a very nifty profit in both good times and bad. Then one day his CEO decided to go to the next level of expansion: ›to conquer‹ eight new countries and double global spending to 40 percent while forming new strategic alliances with at least a dozen first-rate suppliers. There was also a whole bunch of operative goals, running the gauntlet down to reducing packaging costs by 50 percent.

His executive colleagues were enthusiastic; the stock price rose by almost 5 percent, and the press cheered. The CEO proudly announced, »This is a decisive step for us which within a very short time will catapult us into a position of market leadership!« Within half a year, the previous market leader had taken over 3 percent of his share of the market.

What went wrong? The next round of strategy meetings was called and the individual management board members delivered their explanations: »The crisis hit us harder than we thought!«, »Supply chains worldwide are becoming unstable!«, »The rank and file just aren't cooperating.« – »This is no reproach,« says Thorsten Schiefer. »Those are the usual suspicions, and these constraints really do slow such campaigns down. But they are not the SMIF.« The Single Most Important Factor, the monumental snag, the bottleneck.

It is typical for complex problems – and this is what difficulties in global networks usually are: The complexity often keeps you from seeing where the all-important lever is. The problem is not that no management board member is able to find a solution. The problem is that *everyone* has a solution, and none of them are really the SMIF. »It is not because the management board does not see clearly enough,« believes Schiefer. »It requires a Nestor role.«

If you pay close attention to your Homer, you will notice with astonishment that Nestor, in spite of his phenomenal successes and perfect networking, always managed to remain an outsider. According to Schiefer, »What first seems to be a drawback is actually the incredible benefit of a Nestor: He doesn't really belong somewhere. He's not going round in circles with everybody else because he's not inside the circle. He does not lose the overview in the heat of battle because he's standing outside of the turmoil. That's why he can see what no one involved in the struggle can see.«

The only problem is that those in the middle of the turmoil forget to summon their Nestor. In the case of the English investment goods manufacturers, the group of strategists met half a dozen times, went round in circles, got on each others' nerves and lost weeks of valuable time before the CEO finally called upon the spirit of his forefather Ulysses and dialed the hotline.

The Nestor hotline

These days, Nestors come in packs: For an entire week, a team of three Nestors had a look around the strategy implementing areas of the company. After two days the team could see where the problem lay. The management board's expansion strategy was well-advised, practical, sensible, carefully thought out, equipped with sufficient resources, scarcely touched by the crisis, not limited by upheavals in supply chains and (contrary to the wishes of some board members) 80 percent of the employees were taking part in it. The catch – and therefore the SMIF – was that the expansion strategy just couldn't get off the ground.

Even at the operative level it is clear to the procurement buyers that they need to reduce packaging costs by half. They also know their usual supplier-squeezing tactics alone won't make that possible. Some of them even recognize that they must also forge strategic alliances, strategic partnerships, or at least mutual optimization projects with the suppliers. But only about 10 out of 170 corporate purchasers and supply chain managers are familiar with initiating such joint efforts, keeping them on track, and agreeing upon them in a way that they actually function without being sabotaged because of mutual distrust a few months later. Only those ten have the know-how, the experience and the proven project success records. Unfortunately, they are totally booked out with other projects. Because for each of these ten competent network managers there are another five or more projects.

A typical Nestor question: What keeps the strategy from working?

This phenomenon of lacking project capacity rides the way up through the project from operative goals to the primary strategic objective: to conquer eight new countries. There are simply not enough competent project managers. The war for talents was lost on this front and has now developed into a bottleneck that is blocking the lofty aims of the management board. Why didn't they see the bottleneck coming?

»It's a self-evident question leading nowhere,« says Thorsten Schiefer. »Why does Ulysses need a Nestor? Caught in the midst of the battle, it is hard to see the wood for the trees. That is not the question.« The question is: If the Ulysses-Nestor team works, why wouldn't a sensible person make use of it? Why would he waste time trying to figure out why it works? It is enough to know that it *does* (if the Nestor has enough network experience).

In the meantime, the English investment goods manufacturer has cleared up their bottleneck problem. They took old projects and reprioritized them, put them on hold or redistributed them so the schedules of the capacities of the ten project leaders with the best network expertise were freed up. In a crash course, they trained 18 high-potential candidates to be first-rate project leaders. And they lured a few more away from competitors. Currently, they are holding the same share of the market as the market leader. An example of the success effect of the Nestor method?

The true question is: How can a management team sit together and not come up with the obvious idea that they lack project leaders for their strategies? Because a management meeting is the last place in the world where such an idea would arise. This is because the very words ›management team‹ are an oxymoron.

›Management team‹ is an oxymoron

Business consultants are frequently berated – often deservedly so – for being arrogant, lacking experience in practice, and only being interested in their exorbitant fees. They leave behind traces of destruction wherever they tinker, they are snobs, cold-blooded and superficial in interpersonal relations. Even if not a single word of this was true, this is their image in the eyes of the public. Unfortunately: Public image does not count for much here. The public does not sit on the management board. The public is not responsible for umpteen thousand employees or million dollar deals. The public does not exhaust itself with this kind of responsibility, so it has the energy to protest loudly when something goes wrong.

A board member who understandably wishes to remain anonymous once confided to me over a coffee break, »I'd rather talk with an overbearing bore about optimizing our network than talk with no one at all about it!« An amazingly human reaction to the more objective problems with networks:

Who can a board member talk to about networks?

Board members, CEOs and other top managers can talk to a lot of people about almost all other business-related subjects. These days, every manager will find interlocutors for the subjects of marketing, sales, production and corporate responsibility. Supply chain lingo, by contrast, the language of globalization, is still only spoken by a handful of eccentrics in procurement and supply chain management. If the topic is networks, these experts can barely talk to anyone because there is (as yet) hardly anyone who speaks ›their language‹. Global networks and the accompanying discipline of supply chain management have not been around long enough for their philosophy to have spread, even within management as a whole.

Put it to the test and talk to a board member, responsible for R&D, about global networks. After a few minutes he or she will be confused and ask you what the difference between supply management and supply chain management is or why the costs for intellectual property rights in global networks are chronically underestimated in relation to the total cost.

Questions like these are true discussion killers. Both parties turn away in relief – and the concerns about the network remain the personal torment of the CPO or head of purchasing who is probably not only sitting below in the depths of the building (see chapter 2) but continues to be misunderstood by the entire world – and nevertheless expected to supply them with jeans from Singapore and tennis shoes from Romania. These network captains have almost no one they can talk to about what needs to be discussed. Almost any married person will understand such communication deficiencies: They might lead to the end. Management is nearly 90 percent communication. No communication, no management – and we will end up with even more toxic Barbie dolls. This is how simply the global networks work if they *do not* work.

At this point in the discussion, a know-it-all business journalist once stopped me to point out that a network board member could at least exchange ideas with his colleagues on the management board team, sharing advice about optimizing the network. What a brilliant idea! What would we do without our wonderful business editors? Of course an in-house team can optimize their network without external support, without a Nestor, all by themselves. Everyone knows that two (or more) heads are better than one, right? The funny thing about that, and only a few actually get it, is: Calling a management board team a ›team‹ is an oxymoron or a contradiction in terms.

Calling a management board team a ›team‹ is an oxymoron.

Management boards are really something. They're a pack of wild and ready guys who view even the most serious business crisis as a challenge rather than a threat. They are ambitious and competitive, and in the dark recesses of their minds, they think of only one thing (success – what else?). Yes, management boards are something and can be many things, but a team is not what they are. Not if global networks are at stake. These are (still) in a shaky condition, so a team discussion ›at the highest level‹ would inevitably lead to almost every single member of the management board having to admit his own oversights, weaknesses, gaps in knowledge and interface mishaps to the network management. And that isn't going to happen for understandable reasons.

If networks are discussed at all, it is not in order to work as a team on finding optimum solutions; it is to show one's dear colleagues in the poorest possible light. This is not absurd; this is management. And I'd like to see the guy dim-witted enough to complain about it.

Board members have to be competitive to achieve the levels of success to which they aspire. It is what we expect of them today, so we cannot start griping about it tomorrow just because we feel like it and because the supply chain in the automobile industry breaks down.

Solutions via Nestor.

If a network problem cannot be solved by the (management board) team, a Nestor is required. And that is what is going to happen. During the current economic crisis, the budgets traditionally targeted for cuts plummeted straight down to the cellar the way they usually do in a crisis: advertising, training, consulting, travel, office equipment, investments. Training, investments and consultation dealing with optimizing the network went against this trend and were passionately sought after – ruining Christmas 2008 for many trainers, consultants and academic workers (see chapter 1).

By the way, all traces of Nestor are lost in Homer's baroquely tangled tale. The epic storyteller lets us know that Ulysses eventually made it home to Ithaca where he smote a horde of suitors with his bow and arrow who were harassing his faithfully waiting wife, and lived to a ripe old age before gently departing this world in unparalleled fame and honor. We hear about the hardly more violent end met by the Greek king Agamemnon in his bathroom. But what we do not learn is how, when and where Nestor came to meet his maker. So, it might not be unreasonable to imagine he is still out there making the rounds, whispering his wise advice to the greatest strategists, and gently leading them out of obscurity and on to truly legendary successes. Such as, for example, our next candidates from Best Practice.

Waltzing to the networks

The German producer of laboratory equipment literally started out in his father's workshop. Thanks to intense specialization, the company has grown immensely since and is presently represented in quite a few countries. At the beginning of the current economic crisis, the CPO took the opportunity to bring his international network up to speed. »We have to reduce costs even further. And we scarcely use even half of our supply chain's potential.« The concept he came up with has three steps like a waltz:

- Personnel development
- Network development
- Procurement development

Actually, these three topics always come up when network controls need to be optimized. But somehow these three points usually end up in an unfortunate conglomerate and are dealt with in a uniform and undifferentiated manner. Afterwards the managing board ask themselves why instead of gliding along like a waltz their network is still staggering about like a drunken sailor. It is because things have been thrown together that should have been treated separately:

- We want better control of our networks? Then we must bring our people up to speed. Personnel development.
- We want better coordinated, more efficient, risk-transparent, supplier-flexible and crisis-secure networks the role of which in the success of the company is immediately clear to even the trainees in the controlling program? Then we must modify the structures and coordination processes in the network to become more efficient, more crisis secure, less expensive, et cetera. Network development.
- We want to integrate our central control unit (which used to be »purchasing«) into the value creation chain (which up to now has been occupied by the specialized departments) and ensure that well-trained employees can actually accomplish their appointed task of network guidance? Then we must have the people in »purchasing« acquiring the competency they will need in order to secure their acceptance in each of the specific departments that have shown scepticism in the past. Procurement development.

If your head is spinning from the suddenly exploding complexity of the subject matter, this is exactly why it is usually better to have external support to help with this triad of subjects. For this reason, the laboratory equipment manufacturer hired a consulting team before their network pilots were asked to ›dance‹. The first step they were advised to do is a surprising one.

Typical!

The human factor influences complex networks more than assumed.

Who is to blame for the current economic crisis? If I ask five economists, I will get six explanations. Not that fundamental mathematical impossibility is surprising but a point that up to now has been overlooked in public discussion as well as by management: What economists have to offer are *economic* reasons. What if the crisis has other, non-economic causes? For example, greed, pride, arrogance, incompetency and herd mentality?

The human factor influences complex networks a lot more than has so far been assumed or, more importantly, taken into consideration. We ought to know this already because in our global networks we deal daily with the fatal consequences of that connection. As an example, the head supply chain manager of a French investment goods company reports the following incident: »When we were projecting the current new works, we wanted to discuss transmission, materials and the selection of components relatively early on. The Americans on the team refused to talk about it and instead just kept going off on abstract flights of rapture over the product's allegedly fantastic possibilities and market chances. We lost weeks on time to market because of the Americans!« Is that frustrating? That's the way it is in networks.

Friction in networks may be caused by culture clash but also by incompatibility among individuals.

Networks are often inefficient. Networks are usually erratic. Networks much too often cause crises in companies and economy. From time to time, they get so busy with internal struggles that they cannot perform their real job of increasing company value. Busy? More like handicapped. But we are doing something about it! We are booking cross-cultural training sessions! Unfortunately, that is only half the battle.

Since the prejudices against ›those Americans‹, ›those Germans‹, ›those Russians‹ and other nationalities have been around for so long, science has had a chance to study them. The results are amazing: The differences between the individual nations are there and can be smoothed over by cross-cultural training. But the differences between cultures are fewer than the differences between different types of people. A British creative person, for example, is much more similar to a German creative person than he is to a British man of action. This makes sense, for if the conflicts in networks were due merely to nationality there was no conflict within purely national networks. But there is ... definitely! Ergo: Friction and inefficiency in networks are strongly linked to the fact that it is difficult for individuals of different personality types to get along with each other.

This is precisely what the French supply chain manager mentioned above failed to recognize. He thought he had trouble with »les Américains foutus«, but he simply had a problem with visionaries – because he and most of his French developer colleagues are of the personality type that loves to delve into detail. (He overlooked the fact that the few French visionaries on his team got along very well with the whimsical Americans, by the way – because he himself is such a detail person!)

Typological knowledge for better network guidance

With some basic typological knowledge quantum leaps in effectiveness, precision, and durability of network guidance can be achieved. Nestors know this and explain it at their coaching assignments. Unfortunately, up to now only a few of their charges have been listening. Let's take this German laboratory equipment manufacturer, for example. The company conscientiously planned a basic education course in typology to be completed before starting its ›fitness course‹ on network-specific topics from cost analysis and risk management to strategic sourcing. The part that sounds esoteric is based upon one of the oldest philosophical principles of classical antiquity.

Nosce te ipsum

This was written on the Temple of Apollo at Delphi, »Know thyself«. Why should you? Because you wouldn't make a fool of yourself like the Frenchman did … and like thousands of network pilots do repeatedly, all day, every day, even today.

Networks are made up of people. The better these people get along with each other, the better they function.

Networks are made up of people. The better these people get along with each other, the better the networks function. In other words, »It's a people's business!«, as EBS President Christopher Jahns never gets tired of emphasizing. Hardly anyone understands what he means. The laboratory equipment manufacturer showed some courage when they integrated a typological pre-training course into their fitness program, and this courageous move proved its worth, first of all to the participants themselves.

They were instantly and spontaneously enthusiastic. That makes sense, because every human being would like to get to know themselves better as long as they can be in an atmosphere free of embarrassment where they feel worthwhile and appreciated. And everyone would like to get to know their colleagues better, the ones they never really understood or always thought of as difficult, opinionated or overly eager.

Conflicts and frictions which have been going on for years often disappear in seconds because of the aha-experience.

People with good knowledge of human nature get along a lot better with each other. This pleasant side-effect even led Americans in certain circles to put their personality type on their name tag or have it printed on their business cards. In meeting-and-greeting situations, this often leads to a hello: »You're an extroverted detail worker? So am I! Great!« OK, we do not have to copy this method, but typology certainly brings about identification and a sense of community, a network within a network, so to speak.

All that is important to know is that people only understand each other better if they are able to know themselves in the first place. If you don't recognize your own behavioral predispositions (character or personality type) in the long run. you are just holding yourself back because your quirks are getting on everyone's nerves – everyone, that is, who does not share your behavioral predispositions.

If all the different types within a network – the visionaries and the actionaries, the cerebral and the physical, those who want to plan everything well in advance and those who want to leave all options open until the very last minute (for anyone interested, that is MBTI typology) – finally stop their endless quarrelling because they have learned to perceive and discern their own typical behavioral characteristics as well as those of their partners, then networks usually take a quantum leap in their productivity and working climate ... and in their resistance to crisis.

It does not matter much which form of typology you use. MBTI, the Myers-Briggs Type Indicator, is popular internationally because it is scientifically validated, reliable and easy to use. It harks back to C. G. Jung and is widespread and understood in all countries of the world. In Europe, DISG, H.D.I., Insight and others are widely used – and there are many others.

If you are now impatiently drumming your fingers on your desk, you are not only giving yourself away as a detail-oriented person of action, you are also well within your rights. What can all this typology business do for our laboratory equipment manufacturer?

Know your enemy

Sun Tzu, the Chinese strategist, often stated how important it is to know your enemy inside and out. The same is true for friends, relatives, superiors and network partners. Let's integrate the basic typological training into our triad of elements:

Personnel development

Typology is the turbo charger for every behavioral technique.

It is good if supply chain managers go into negotiations training, for example, and learn to negotiate better so they can cut expenses even more. But what do they learn there? Not a single negotiating technique will work without typological knowledge of human nature and character. This is actually one of the reasons why half of all educational funds are wasted: Participants go out and blindly apply the techniques they learned without any consideration of character type, much to the annoyance of their counterpart. Any technique is a total flop when it comes to the human factor. Here's the catch: 80 percent of specialized trainers do not even know this.

I constantly come into contact with managers – even management boards – purchasers, network pilots and supply chain managers who make technical errors when negotiating or applying the correct techniques, but in the wrong way. Yet due to their typological x-ray vision (as a result of good training!), they are excellent judges of character and wrap their negotiation partners around their fingers.

Network development

Knowledge of human nature is stronger than technique. Used together, they work even better.

When CPOs talk about optimizing their networks, they talk about structures, processes, budgets, responsibilities, competency, and organization. What they do not talk about is the commonplace fact that their current networks are at least partly in a sub-optimal condition because the network partners just won't get along with each other. Like outdated light bulbs, 60 percent of their energy is expended not for their raison d'être (light), but in frictional heat. They argue or do not cooperate efficiently. More likely, they simply do not work *side by side*, but at the most *parallel to* one another or even explicitly and implicitly *against* one another.

We deal with globalization every day, but we still haven't realized the human dynamic.

In our former national networks it didn't always work out on the human level. But somehow, people got it together. In globalized networks, on top of typological conflict we also have a culture clash. Suddenly the problem reaches a critical mass and explodes. In globalized networks, a manager should no longer try to get by without typological tools.

Procurement development

If purchasers complain about their lack of acceptance by the specialized divisions, then it is certainly at least partly a problem of the purchasers' lack of expertise to talk with the divisions about their specialized fields. But this is actually a minor neglect.

I know a lot of network pilots who have a general understanding of purchasing but still get along really well with the engineers in the company, are held in their esteem and invited to their meetings. Why? One of them explained: »You just have to know how to talk to engineers! They don't expect you to know the hardness of a safety cotter-pin measured by the Rockwell method. They only expect you to let them explain the Rockwell method to you – and then to learn pretty quickly as you go along.«

If a network pilot pays attention to the experts in the specialized departments, they will accept him.

If a buyer wants to gain even more acceptance, he should start reading about typology. And just in case you are still sceptical you should know that your scepticism is shared by all those whose jobs involve dealing with people full-time – doctors, salespeople, customer consultants, fathers and mothers. Are we not getting upset about these people day by day because in spite of all their expertise, when it comes to dealing with people they have no idea? Do you want to be just like the people you get so upset about?

Naturally, with such an x-ray vision into the human psyche there is danger of abuse and manipulation. For example, if the French we mentioned above had realized that their American counterparts were striking examples of visionaries who didn't really go in for excessive detail and splitting hairs, they could have slipped any detail right past them – they wouldn't even have noticed! Yet this is something people with a (well-trained!) knowledge of human nature will never do because they know that every manipulation will backfire at some point – leaving the shrapnel to hit the one who let it off. Not to mention the fact that networks will break apart sooner or later anyway if the partners are so afraid of manipulation that they communicate merely on a tactical basis.

At a glance: A strategic ally

- Network management is so new and, because of the dynamics of globalization, so complex that internal management teams are very often taken to the very limits of their competency.
- Best Practice managers overstep these bounds by bringing in external network specialists.
- Tip: Since the discipline is rather new, supply chain specialists should be preferred to more generalized consultants.
- Tip: All training should be preceeded by a short basic training in typology. Unless you are skilled at dealing with yourself and others you will not be able to implement any further techniques.
- Supply chain optimization should be based upon three points: personnel development, network development and procurement development.

11 Develop Leaders!

»Tell me, oh Critias, how can a man choose his leader? Would he not choose a person who had developed discipline in himself, well aware that each of his decisions originating from fear, pride, or vanity, would have a thousandfold effect on those being led?«
Plato

The globalization trap

It's the spring of 2009. The global financial crisis is on the rampage and cost pressures have companies in a strangle hold. A few German companies buy a total of 150 tons of Indian scrap metal. A typical ›low cost country‹ deal.

In the middle of an increasing shortage of raw material and escalations in commodity prices, the deal is a real bargain. The metal is of good quality, the delivery is on time, and everyone is happy – until someone has the crazy idea to put a Geiger counter on the scrap metal. He runs for his life. The ›bargain‹ is sending out rays like a neon light. It's radioactive.

At this point the scrap metal has already been distributed to several German regions. The authorities ring the alarm bells. The media misses out on this coup because they are overwhelmed by the globalization avalanche. The army considers the emergency deployment of ABC-SE and decontamination units. Technically, there has been an atomic assault on German soil – in times of peace. Well, these things happen. Poisonous Barbie dolls, explosive mortgages, radioactive scrap metal. It's no big thing. It's just part of your everyday globalization accident situation, isn't it?

Most globalization accidents are not accidents at all.

It starts with a poisoned Barbie doll and ends up with Iceland and Hungary being bankrupt. And in between you have the odd nuclear accident. I am not saying that these so-called accidents *might* happen. I am saying that they *have to* happen. The global networks will continue to produce them with horrifying regularity. Why?

The leadership crisis

Let's first look at the obvious cause of the accident: the buyers. How could they buy radioactive scrap metal, for God's sake? Were they being careless? Was it on purpose? Or criminal negligence?

In fact, it was quite the opposite. I am absolutely sure that the buyers of the radioactive scrap metal were highly competent and thinking in the backs of their mind: »Why on earth are these Indians selling their scrap metal so cheaply? There's something rotten in the state of Denmark!« And I am also sure that they immediately thought of Gutenberg next (the business guru): »But how can I reach my incredibly high cost saving targets if I worry about every bargain that comes along?«

Because at the time when this radioactive scrap metal was being purchased, every respectable company in this financial crisis was checking each and every procurement contract for possible savings down to the last cent. No right-minded buyer would have said no to a bargain like that – not if he wanted to keep his job.

Most accidents are evidence of a leadership gap in the system.

Accidents such as the radioactive scrap metal don't point to the buyer having a problem. They point to a real leadership deficit in the networks: We expect buyers to not only buy, but to manage networks on the side. Wishful thinking at its best. A traditionally selected and trained buyer has a lot of skills. He has expertise and process competence, he is good at calculating and knows how to negotiate. But that does not make him a leader. A leader would not have radioactive scrap metal allowed into his network because, for example, he would have had competence in risk management.

This means being able to quickly identify the risk attached with every transaction in a network and weigh the costs against the anticipated benefit. He would have had the necessary tools and would have worked with external risk agents, such as university professors and consultants. He would have done this because he did not only have training in purchasing but in leadership as well.

Shortly after the scandal (which never made it into the public eye), one of these network leaders explained to me: »We were offered the scrap metal, too. I called my Indian contact in the raw materials market and she told me that the Indian scrap metal dealer had just finished purchasing on a grand scale from Russia. And that in Russia a few military nuclear plants had been dismantled. And that a few tons of the stuff were floating around that couldn't be accounted for. That was a bit too risky for me to mess with.«

The current financial crisis is also a leadership crisis: The persons in charge don't have enough risk competence.

Networks need to be led. One of the required leadership skills is risk competence. Another has to do with something that powers the engines of managers.

The fuel of leaders

What motivates people? What motivates purchasers who buy radioactive scrap metal? It's their pay checks, in other words, their operational performance target: reducing costs. And this is what they did – no doubt. This is the built-in »Sollbruchstelle«, as they say in German, meaning a predetermined breaking point. We owe this term to the current financial crisis:

Anyone agreeing to a two-digit rate of return with a banker shouldn't be surprised when he comes up with the great idea to create ›scrap‹ credit in a saturated market. He had no other choice to reach his performance targets. Everybody puts the blame on bankers. However, they were and are just the willing instruments of incentive systems getting wildly out of control. Critics of capitalism want to get rid of this system for precisely this reason. However, there is an easier and more obvious way: Not all bankers dealt with ›scrap‹ products. Not all bankers were motivated by short-term operational targets.

We cannot give people certain targets and then complain when they pursue them.

If you just cringed, I'm not surprised: The term has become little more than jargon at best. At worst, it is completely misunderstood. It is commonly supposed to

Leaders motivate themselves by responsibility.

describe responsibility for employees and for performance targets which takes away a lot of its value: This disciplinary and business responsibility could quite definitely be applied to those who created the toxic mortgage funds, too. Yet it didn't stop them from behaving irresponsibly.

Responsibility refers to moral responsibility.

Accountability and moral responsibility are not only completely different things, on a purely empirical basis they actually have a negative influence: Some people are so blinded by the radiance of their own responsibilities for employees and business figures that they act with an unbelievable overestimation of their own abilities in an irresponsible way. More to the point: They mistake power for responsibility.

When I ask purchasers what they would have done in the radioactive scrap metal situation, they answer with more or less justifiable indignation: »Of course no one wants to buy radioactive scrap metal. But I'm not always able to tell whether there is a nuclear bomb behind a good deal!« That's right. However, leaders will answer the same question differently. Most say: »Of course I have to cut costs, too, and get my numbers down. But when an offer is that cheap, I know I have to take a closer look – savings or not.« This is true responsibility: in an ethical sense. And now the million dollar question: How can we get these responsibly thinking and acting leaders as quickly as possible to lead our networks?

Born to lead

The old adage that some people are »naturally born leaders« unfortunately still rules executive suites today. This assumption very beautifully illustrates an otherwise non-justifiable claim to power. However, it does not help to fill the leadership gap:

There are no naturally born leaders. Leaders have to be developed.

Where? At business schools, for example. They are being accused at the moment of helping to create the current financial crisis because of their negligent and amoral training of managers. Even if the accusation was true, there is no reason to get rid of business schools but rather a call for companies in the process of recruiting to take a closer look at the applicants coming from the business schools. If you check their applicants for moral and ethical strength, you will be surprised.

Some graduates are simply unable to talk about morals in management from a normative point of view. Yet there are others who can not only talk about it but have already proven ethical responsibility during their studies in the different projects they worked on. Those are the leaders who wouldn't buy scrap mortgage funds or radioactive scrap metal because they could not live with the responsibility of the negative consequences.

Not all graduates of renowned schools are the same. There are clear differences when it comes to a fundamental moral constitution. You only have to open your eyes and thoroughly grill your applicants. If one of them doesn't know what a Supply Chain Code of Conduct is but knows how to coherently and believably answer the typical morally weighted questions, this person is demonstrating a stable moral leadership potential. Assuming that your recruitment can really check the moral appropriateness of candidates with the proper questions and tests. Can it?

Not all graduates of renowned schools are the same.

What is true for former education is also true for an MBA and EMBA: If you are going to hire an MBA graduate or pay for an EMBA, then at least choose a business school where the moral training of future leaders is not just words on paper. At the European Business School, for example, the current class of MBA graduates worked together with their company partner, Danone, to bring yoghurt from Bangladesh to Malawi. Not for those consumers who could afford a luxury product like yoghurt in a country rampant with starvation but for those who really couldn't afford it, but needed it for the basic fulfillment of vitamin and mineral needs. Graduates like these understand more than just the theory behind Corporate Social Responsibility. They will also be able to lead projects which might as well make a profit for the project company. It doesn't really matter to me which business school a graduate comes from as long as he had an ethically based education.

It is crucial that the candidates are not starting at ›zero‹ in my company when it comes to moral leadership. Leaders with the necessary sense of responsibility will find it very difficult to buy radioactive scrap metal, or deal in rotten mortgage funds. It is not only moral but financially viable.

Of course leadership is not merely about moral and risk management competence. A network leader must be able to manage his networks from a technical point of view, too. He must be able to analyse it with appropriate instruments and optimize it in no time. A network leader can masterfully reduce the excessive complexity in networks and find solutions while others are still working on the problems. He is a master of the pragmatic and of building relationships. He can motivate, excite and manage people across interfunctional teams, helping them to reach their goals as easily as possible. He can do this better than any manager relying exclusively on disciplinary force. We all know this won't help anyway. It won't help either to talk for hours about a catalog of characteristics of the ideal leader. This won't lead anywhere. The only important matter left is: Where can we find them?

Where do leaders come from?

This is no trivial question if you consider that all great philosophers, thinkers, and pedagogues in the history of mankind, along with our own parents and teachers, have failed at it. They've imparted a lot of capabilities to us, leadership skills, however, weren't among them. And if they were, it was more or less at random. How can companies solve a problem in which so many others failed?

With seminars, of course. Leadership skills are being preached in every reliable general management training course. It's important to get to know the conventional tools. However, experience shows: A seminar won't create any leaders. Otherwise we would be sending all of our politicians to seminars regularly. If training courses are able to train the fundamentals, but don't lead to the end result, what will help instead? You really ought to be able to figure that out on your own by now.

Which of the many instruments discussed in this book is the most suitable to form leaders? I know you said »coaching«. One-to-one coaching over several months is ideal for that. And anyone talking about coaching will have to mention »mentoring« as well. When I talk to experienced leaders, they always describe the profound influence some mentor had on them at a certain point. This doesn't necessarily mean an official mentoring program. In many cases it isn't. Good mentors pick their protégés themselves: A real leader wants to pass his life's work to a chosen few. And vice versa: Anyone longing to become a true leader will always be looking for someone in the company to act as a mentor. A clever board member will encourage this kind of initiative diplomatically.

Encouraging mentoring encourages leadership development.

A CPO of my acquaintance always asks his high potentials: »Have you got a mentor yet?« He regularly has every top manager in his ranks talk about their mentees, their worries and their progress. Asking is leading. His message is: Mentoring is important to me!

A mid-sized company with an unambiguous Supply Chain Code of Conduct shows how mentoring will strengthen the leadership skills of potential candidates: »We don't work with companies who use child labor.« One of their supply managers had just found an Asian supplier who definitely employed adults only, even if the conditions were rather poor. An average supply manager would have closed this case. He or she would have given the go-ahead. The supply manager in this case hesitated.

She talked to her mentor about her doubts: »The supplier doesn't pay minimum wage – which actually doesn't exist yet for this industry in this country. However, I still don't feel good about it.« Her mentor listened to the background of the story attentively and then gave her some advice: »No one here is going to give you a bad time if you give the contract to this supplier. However, in a year you'll feel bad about it. None of us can escape our scruples. It's not healthy. But don't get rid of the supplier immediately. Talk to them once or twice. If you can make them believe that you are looking for a long-term partnership, perhaps they'll raise their employee salaries because they know they're having a return on investment.« This is precisely what the supplier did after a few detailed discussions. Later, the mentee said, »I learned that a leader cannot afford to ignore his conscience. It actually pays off in the end, for everyone. But you really need a lot of courage to do so.« She probably would not have managed to achieve this far-reaching insight on her own.

Every leader has a mentor at some point.

Why do so few companies make use of mentoring? Because they expect that an adequate supply of leaders will fly in through the company windows from the business schools? Fully trained and in sufficient number? This is not only naïve, it's totally unrealistic. Even if the business schools could achieve this: Only continuous development can turn a new graduate into a stable leader. In addition to the mentor, the coach is another ›development helper‹ in creating leaders.

Leadership coaching

Very few companies have a sufficient amount of suitable mentors. This is another reason for coaching: A coach is a kind of paid-for external mentor with special development expertise. Coaching forms leaders amazingly faster and more effective if the coach is good, that means if he brings his own management and network experience, if possible, and is not just an expert in his field. And if the CPO who has hired him asks him to put his coaching focus on leadership development. This focus is a key factor: Of course we all have plenty of other things to do. However, it takes a bit of extra time to develop the leaders in demand.

The companies you have gotten to know in this book followed exactly this development pathway. They didn't complain about the universities educating not enough leaders. They developed them on their own. There is obviously no hard and fast rule for this. I have only one cautionary advice: No rules, gurus, or textbooks may define what a leader is made of. It always depends on the individual company and situation.

On that note, let's consider the example of an American textile corporation which took over a huge supplier in an emerging market. Something happened which often occurs with takeovers: The workforce which had been taken over felt threatened. A few feared losing their jobs, others fought openly against the textile corporation's company culture. This corporation actually has a very large leadership pool. Their leaders are able to handle their networks, to integrate new company parts quickly into the supply chain, and to deal with any new projects on a high level of project management competency. However, in this concrete situation, their wonderful leadership skills were of not much use. There was only one thing that really mattered: the current leaders' lack of integration skills. Even 14 months after the takeover some of the individual departments of the subsidiary were still more or less fighting against the parent company.

A leader will never be finished.

Normally, companies will increase the pressure on those being taken over in this situation. Or they push them away, like Adidas pushed Salomon away when it emerged that the two company cultures would never get along. The US textile corporation chose a different way. They realized that their leaders needed to improve their integration skills and invited them to a workshop in which the integration skills of each were identified and rated. The participants then received individual coaching sessions based on their leadership development potential. Integration projects were set up in which the leaders worked together closely with their coaches over the following months. Two years after the takeover, the new subsidiary was finally realizing the profit which had been the reason for the takeover in the first place:

Filling the leadership skills gap always generates the highest benefit.

The current crisis is evidence of this fact. Or as Christian Rast, CEO of BrainNet, says: »We don't have a financial or economic crisis. We have a responsibility crisis.« Entire industries have completely lost their customers' trust because their managers didn't take their responsibilities seriously – suddenly an awareness of responsibility is the leadership skill of the day! Large groups of customers are turning their backs on certain banks. Not because their fortunes were no longer safe there, but because they have lost their faith in the banks. And that is not only true for the banking sector.

Andreas Rutz, for example, CPO of Vattenfall Europe, told the German procurement magazine *Beschaffung aktuell*: »Vattenfall is recognized by its suppliers as a reliable partner.« That means: Vattenfall will continue to receive deliveries. This can no longer be taken for granted in times of breakdowns in the supply chain. If companies are considered unreliable they will soon be left high and dry. But the Swedish energy supply firm always treated their suppliers responsibly. Suddenly, responsible behavior is the most important factor in the economy.

Many companies are out of practice when it comes to leadership development. Communication and project competence, for example, are among the oldest leadership skills, yet too few leaders really master them. Just think how much more difficult it will be now for companies to bring home the concept of a sense of responsibility to their management staff! And to make a difference in the crisis as quickly as possible:

Personnel development is important. Leadership development is even more important.

What every company really needs is a talent factory or leadership school. It doesn't matter what form it takes. It might be a Leadership School or a module in a Supply Chain Academy curriculum, perhaps just a fireside talk.

The CPO of a certain supplier located in the Alps reports: »I invite my leadership team once a month to sit with me by the fire. We organize catering and enjoy a few hours together in pleasant conversation. At least that's what it appears to be. I use the opportunity to listen intently to the personal culture of communication of each person. Which virtues are important to them? How strong are their feelings of responsibility for the company? And I try to give unobtrusive tips.« If the person doesn't put these tips into practice, he or she will not be invited to the fireplace again – another person will take his or her place as a future leader. That is surely one of the easiest ways to implement leadership development.

It is astonishing that the CPO himself takes the time to develop his future and current leaders. He doesn't delegate this task. Sometimes he would send a candidate to a coach. However, he is still holding the reins in the process. That's why his company is recognized as one of the best talent factories. It generates more true leaders than all competitors put together.

At a glance: Leadership in networks

- Not every network breakdown means there is a skills gap. Chronic deficiencies point to a gap in leadership.
- Leadership is not defined by accountability, it is defined by responsibility.
- Leaders are not born, or appointed, they are developed.
- Leadership coaching is a potential development path for leaders.
- A leader is never finished, there is always a leadership skill which needs to be strengthened.

12 Wild, wild West

Black Bart Bolton

When Charles Bolton appeared on the scene, ladies fainted, babies cried and grown men shook in fear like little children. Bolton, nick-named ›Black Bart‹ was every horse's nightmare but an uncannily successful businessman when it came to robbing stagecoaches. In fact he was one of the most famous in the wild West, and the terror of Wells Fargo, the then biggest logistics company for the transport of valuables of the day.

Bolton had racked up about 30 holdups by the year 1880. Mostly successful but amazingly all by himself! He chose the Wells Fargo stagecoaches, because they not only transported mail and passengers, they carried money and precious metals as well: They were the ones who hauled the gold from the dusty mines of the Sierra Nevada, distributing it to the companies who carried out the processing and finishing work. In purely monetary terms, Wells Fargo could easily have survived the losses incurred by the stagecoach robberies. 30 robbed transports were nothing in comparison to the huge annual transportation volume of the safest logistics company of the day.

It was the tremendous loss to their image that hurt much more than the financial loss – who would put their trust in a logistics company that regularly lost its freight to a rebellious backwoods countryman in such a spectacular way? The scandal was made all the worse by the fact that Black Bart not only robbed, but rhymed as well. And with a special talent for iamb and trochee.

After every successful robbery, he put his six-shooter revolver away, in favor of a quill, leaving a self written poem, in which he styled himself as the Robin Hood of the West and Wells Fargo as the lyrical idiot. He robbed according to his own poet's ethos, not for himself, but for all: for the oppressed worker and the underpaid cowboy out on the range, for the little guy. He quickly won the public's sympathy and the media, along with the little guy, who could identify with the swashbuckling lone fighter, even though he was a notorious outlaw. When Bolton was finally caught after years of unchallenged looting, it had more to do with his getting on in years than the talent of his pursuers.

Bolton had grown old. The judge at the time of the trial gave him six years of prison, but let him go early in 1887 because of his advancing years. His words could not be affirmed, however, it was said that the judge justified this action as not wanting to punish an old man just because a bunch of young guys weren't able to protect their supply chain against risks. But the young guys hit back. In a way that is still earning their company respect today. Wells Fargo paid back Bolton for his successes in robbing their company in a paradoxical way.

The company's risk manager, who had never been able to control the one man risk Bolton in his active days, had the brilliant idea, once Bolton had been released, to remove the unique threat once and for all through effective risk management: They paid the desperado a very handsome, life long pension. They asked of him only one small thing in return: never to rob a stagecoach again. The old bandit gave his amused consent and lived to a ripe old age as a living legend in an orderly and above all legal fashion. His name is still written in the history books of today. The names of the ingenious risk managers at Wells Fargo are nowhere to be found. Which is a shame. I would have loved to find out more about them. Their ingeniousness is needed more than ever today.

Because times are changing. And not necessarily for the better. When it comes to the safety and security of supply chains, things have actually gotten a lot worse, so much so that some people long for the days of the wild West again. Back then the supply risks were at least recognizable at first glance as an obvious risk: When Black Bart Bolton galopped around the bend with a bandana over his face and a revolver swinging in his hand, the risk was apparent to everyone.

The modern risks in our global networks, on the other hand, are almost invisible. And a lot more dangerous. They require cleverer ideas than paying out a pension to shut out a risk factor.

Risk!

Anyone thinking about the risks in supply networks usually thinks about the symbol of modern risk management, the poisoned barbie. Or the poisonous milk powder or the pesticides in clothing. What can board members do other than laugh at such risks: those are one-offs, the exceptions and huge breakdowns that the media love to make fun of. Because they know next to nothing about the seriousness of daily risks in routine network management. Let's take a look at a risky situation, from the world of real life risk management.

The supply manager of an English company decides that he wants to start getting category ›X‹ goods globally as soon as possible. In spite of the economic downturn, it isn't that easy to find the right suppliers in the relatively overheated emerging markets. One of them in particular manages to impress the responsible strategic sourcer: His documents look »absolutely fabulous«! All necessary certificates and standards have been fulfilled, there are very humane working conditions, they have documented good quality measures and references are OK. The sourcer checks the offer with a fine-tooth comb. He's not new to this. He's been in procurement for 15 years. He knows the pitfalls hidden in nicely written offers like the back of his hand. He doesn't find any. So he makes the order and gets the shock of his life.

On the planned day of delivery there is no sign of the delivery at all. The manager sends emails, makes calls, and writes increasingly urgent messages. The delivery doesn't turn up. The supplier offers the usual explanations: problems in production, delays in delivery from their own suppliers, unexpected bottlenecks in material availability. Finally, the strategic sourcer begins to think something fishy is going on. He forgets about the delivery for a moment and now asks questions about the production process. He may be ›only‹ a purchaser, but he begins to realize that his rudimentary understanding of production processes for category ›X‹ goods is a lot more comprehensive than the person responsible for production for the Asian supplier.

The politely reserved Englishman finally loses his patience in the fifth telephone conversation and asks quite openly why the supplier had promised things in his offer that his production team could never have managed under such conditions. And then the bomb drops: »But that isn't our offer, I copied that from a competitor because it sounded so good.« In answer to the British's angry question of how in the world he could have dared to be so dishonest, the salesman answers in a righteously indignant tone of voice: »Well, how else would we have received your order?« This happens more often than you might think. Anyone who sources globally these days, has a wealth of such problems to report on. When the Supply Chain Management Institute holds workshops at their foreign locations in China, India or Russia, for purchasers, for example, there's no end of stories that come up. Purchasers don't tell these stories to make fun of the situations in the emerging markets. They tell them because they have felt alone in dealing with the circumstances of risk up until now. From academics as well as from their own co-workers and management board:

The risks in supply networks have increased. However, supply chain risk management remains in kindergarten.

It is one of the characteristic indicators of modern network risks, that they are not recognizable at first glance like Black Bart. The above example mentioned an Asian supplier who had falsified an offer, not in the hopes of robbing the Brits, but with the intention, quite consistent with his culture, which the Brit had not recognized, or at least not fully enough, as a risk factor. In the Asian's country the maxim of the past century had been »First get the order. Worry about how to fulfill it later.« Anyone who considers this a thing of the past, never did business with or in the USA. The current President was voted in partly as a result of the saying

»Yes we can!«, because that is the motto of the nation. First put forth a bold assertion, make a claim or send the message – we'll take care of the implementation later. The average US contractor assumes implicitly that he will somehow get the order done, and then boastfully promises this to his potential client. Western Europeans, such as the Germans, calculate and construct until everything is complete from beginning to end before making an offer. But that isn't the point.

The point is, that the British didn't even have the possibility of the plagiarism risk within the offer on their radar. And they didn't have a screening tool on the back burner, with which they could have checked out the risk. When the Chief Financial Officer accuses purchasing of just this fact, the responsible strategic sourcer says: »Excuse me, please, but how could I have detected the fraud? Should I have flown there and visited the supplier in person? Since the financial crisis, our travelling budget has been cut. How can I manage risks properly, when I'm not even allowed to fly?« That pushes the knife a bit farther into the wound.

Modern risk management is about organizational conditions.

The board can continue to instruct its supply managers to check new suppliers down to the last detail. If they don't have any travelling budget, the exercise is pretty useless. Problems such as these are symptomatic of the current situation in supply chain risk management (SCRM). However, in dealing with the problem, normal practice is pretty much on its own.

Supply Chain Risk Management

What academia and textbooks have to say about how to bring the concept of supply chain risk management to the man in the frontlines is not particularly helpful. It sometimes comes across like an unintentional joke. To quote an example: »A supply chain risk is a risk, whose estimated damage in relation to the probability of occurrrence, effects more than one company in the supply chain at the time of its occurrence.« So much for the text book definition. I threw this text book into the recycling bin after reading the quote. Because at this high level the discussion on risks in the global networks, at the moment, is quite sweeping. What would the British strategic sourcer most likely say to me if I held this definition under his nose?

He would probably say in his typical, understated British way that this definition doesn't help him one iota with his current plagiarism risk. This definition alone would never have helped him recognize the risk more clearly or quickly. What he needs are clearly defined processes and standards for risk management which are also clearly defined in the budget: When should he be visiting a supplier in person? Which suppliers does he need to check for concrete risks such as the plagiarism risk? Which concrete questions does he need to ask? What resources such as databases or local market aficionados are available to him? The British supply manager didn't have these standards and processes. That's why the supply chain risk management was just waiting to happen all these years to the British. Not anymore.

Because luckily the British work in a Best Practice company. The board has now recognized the importance of supply chain risk management. They are also not worried that academia has more or less left them high and dry (although there are a few praiseworthy exceptions). Because they are making up for the lack of academically based concepts and instruments which have been tested in practice, with their own expanded leadership competence (see chapter 11). The CPO says: »That's another reason why we equipped our strategic sourcers with comprehensive leadership competency: so that they can check offers made from places which were no more than swampland yesterday.« That's exactly what the strategic sourcers in Britain are also doing.

They negotiate a very clear agreement with their CPO and the Chief Financial Officer as to what the order value is for a supplier that needs to be visited in person and which ones can be compared by someone locally who knows the market, when it's not possible to travel. That is risk management in action. And it pays for itself in the next big order.

Phantom of the workshop

The next time they wanted to bring a supplier from an emerging market into the portfolio, the strategic sourcer is allowed to travel there. The proud supplier leads him across the company site. The Englishman is impressed. As both parties, including the interpreter, reach the workshop, the purchaser gasps: The alleged workshop is a huge scrap heap! Filled with rusted old metal, engine parts, and discarded appliances. It's more than clear that the workshop will not be suitable for manufacturing anything from the day the contract is signed.

Completely unaffected by the strategic sourcers response, the owner explains that all the scrap will be removed immediately and all the necessary machines assembled – as soon as the contract is signed. »Shouldn't that be the other way around?«, asks the Englishman politely? »Maybe where you come from,« the supplier says disgustedly, »but not here! If I don't get the contract, I'll have bought a lot of expensive machinery for nothing! That's how we always do it.« And he's right. That is the usual practice in that country. Luckily, the Englishman discovers another strange habit before he can do any real damage. Not everyone is this fortunate. In fact, it's usually the exception.

The successes in regional networks have made many people blind to the dangers in the global networks.

This has been confirmed by a study carried out by the Aberdeen Group. They discovered that around 60 percent of international companies experienced financial losses due to interruptions in their global supply chain last year. Compared to local, regional and even national networks, that's a shocking amount. The number of interruptions in the supply chain for these ›little‹ networks is closer to ten percent, in our experience. Paradoxically, that's the reason why the global amount is so shockingly high:

Or put another way: Success can become a source of failure. Take a mid-sized French manufacturer. In the past few years the network manager responsible for propulsion technology had his network of suppliers from France, Belgium, Germany and Italy so well under control that the company management automatically appointed him to the role of global network manager when the board decided to increase their global spending to 25 percent. That was a critical mistake.

Because the regional network manager transferred his recipe for success from his old international network one-to-one into the new, global network. What did you expect? Never change a winning team! Unfortunately, the risk situation in global networks is completely different. For the first time in his life, the newly crowned global network manager failed. One of his new BRIC suppliers stole the ideas from his part of the delivery for the French company, selling it illegally to the competition: The new global network manager had never had anything to do with IPR risk in his old European network, the risk of damaging ›intellectual property rights‹. The damage was several million the first time round! Just because the board believed that it was possible to create a global network manager by decree. You can't!

Risk management alone justifies separate training for the supply chain.

This leads to the question of whether separate training could be given to a ›normal‹ manager at all. Why not just create a project group for supply chain risk management to begin with, that doesn't do anything other than protect against risks? The academic debate continues. One academic thinks that risk and purchasing should never be separated and anyone who purchases should manage the risks of that purchase themselves. The other counters with the fact that a strategic buyer would still be completely overwhelmed by such a task and therefore should be allowed enough time for the risk management part. And while the fight is raging, Best Practice implements its own solution: It doesn't really matter who takes on risk management. The main thing is that it is clearly allocated to a definite position and carried out correctly.

Heads in the sand

The Aberdeen Group looked at a few of the most common risks in supply chains: inadvertent violation of export and import restrictions, price and raw material risks, finance risks with suppliers, quality risks and risks in infrastructure. Anyone working in global networks can confirm that these are the usual risks that one has to deal with on a daily basis. The only problem is – no one's doing it.

Surprisingly, only a third of those companies questioned stated that they actively manage the most frequent risks. Two thirds dealt with the risks only when they arrived, after the baby was already in the frying pan. The ostrich strategy seems to be the most common practice: crisis management instead of risk management. Why? There are a few reasons for this. The one proclaimed most often is the lack of risk awareness. While the risks are exploding, risk awareness is still what it used to be.

Risk awareness is still what it used to be.

Not on the operational level. The British purchasers have definitely noticed that globalization has increased their risks drastically. However, the communication of this increase has somehow not made it to the board yet. They think that it's just one of the ›typical procurement problems‹, just at a global level.

For this reason, anti-risk measures are delegated to the rank and file: »Our purchasing department is taking care of that!« In view of this delegation credo, it's easy to see why supply chain risks such as lead in barbies can take on such threatening dimensions: The rank and file are overwhelmed by this problem! Or put another way: If the board makes itself fit as a change agent for supply chain risk management, meaning that they show the necessary risk awareness, then the anti-risk measures will get pushed forward at a much faster pace.

Many board members dont recognize that they have changed in principle.

At this point in the argumentation, a board member will always have presented me with a new study which proves that the number of companies who have categorized supply chain risk management as ›important‹ or ›very important‹ has doubled in the last few years: »You see!« he crows, »something IS being done!« Sure, without doubt. No contest. However he's forgetting the tendency to split hairs in academia: There's a difference between awareness and commitment.

Board member commitment is necessary for supply chain risk management.

I know of boards, for example, who for years have been nodding their heads and ensuring me beyond a shadow of a doubt that »Supply chain risk management

Risk awareness is necessary. Commitment is sufficient.

is our top priority«. However, not a single board member has volunteered to take an SCRM project under their wing or even outsource this responsibility. Or to quote Charles Handy: »Awareness without commitment is just lip service!« It's not enough to talk about supply chain risk management. One also has to put forward the necessary change projects to deal with it. The most mundane of the projects is a solid training program.

In another chapter (see chapter 2) I mentioned that purchasers and network managers have not necessarily been spoiled for choice in the training courses available which would make them fit for their jobs. And the most neglected topic among all neglected training topics is that of risk management.

Anyone wanting to steer networks needs training in supply chain risk management.

Anyone wanting to steer networks needs training in supply chain risk management. That is the minimum requirement. Every network pilot has to understand his risk instruments and be able to use them. Practice shows that both rarely go together. That may be due to the famous Nuremberg funnel idea – where the teacher only has to pour the material into a student's head.

Whenever I meet former participants from my risk management training, I like to ask: »Are you now the master of the risk tools that you learned about?«

»Yes, of course!«

»Do you also use them?«

»Well, hmmm, actually, not so often ...«

Which means never. And which makes it impossible for me to keep from grinning when I hear boards and trainers preaching that their people are definitely able to master certain tools. But that's not what it's all about, I want to argue. Or rather ask: Are you sure that your people haven't mastered the tools a long time ago and simply aren't using them?

It doesn't help for managers to have mastered the use of tools. They also have to use them.

Why don't they? Because they have other things to do. Because their objectives were packaged with a different focus. For example, cost reduction. That's why purchasers are probably willing to buy radioactive goods (see chapter 11), as long as they are available at a huge discount. It's possible that the radioactive scrap metal purchasers really knew their risk management tools. It's even possible that they could use them *perfectly.* They just didn't. And then even the greatest tools are not enough.

Many purchasers master a surprising amount of risk tools. They just don't use them. Because in practice they not only don't have any opportunity, they are in actual fact given a disincentive. As an experienced buyer once said to me: »Risk tools? Don't get me started on that subject. If you look, you can always find something!« And then they can't meet their cost reduction targets. Mathematically put, purchasers are paralyzed by the fear of finding errors in orders that aren't really there. They throw out an option that they could have taken advantage of. Just because their risk tool avoids the risks where one could easily look the other way. That's another reason for the old saying: »No one needs seminars, but everyone needs solutions.«

If risk management is not rewarded, it won't get done.

Which should be followed by: Half of every training budget is money thrown out the window. And it's exactly that half which is invested in training courses whose contents are later mastered, but not put into practice. For the simple reason: What's rewarded gets done. If risk management is not rewarded, it won't get done.

That's the reason some boards believe that purchasers should be given incentives on the risks: According to this, the purchaser who discovered that the impressive supplier workshop was nothing more than a scrap heap, should have received one percent of the savings in the supplier selection. The analogy to suggestion making is clear: When the employee makes a suggestion on how to avoid risk, he/she should, therefore, receive a bonus.

Man doesn't live by bread alone. He doesn't do everything just for the money.

I think this idea is useful but impracticable for the simplest of all reasons in a market economy: They don't pay. The costs which are reduced by avoiding risks have never been charged. So no reasonably thinking Chief Financial Officer will pay out a premium for this. Which isn't all that bad:

There are a lot of CPOs in Best Practice that don't need money to get their supply managers to do risk management. They use another method. A method which the past 200 pages have been devoted to, and which is rarely seen in practice: leadership. Spontaneously, I was thinking of the purchasing manager who asked her managers in every single meeting during which a new supplier was being considered: »And? What's the risk?« And then she ticked off half a dozen specific questions on specific risks. Woe betide the employee who couldn't answer the questions quickly enough! Because then they would have to go back to the drawing board. That's why her employees and managers have their presentations prepared down to the last detail before opening their mouths: What's respected, is done.

What's respected, is done.

Or more simply: He who questions, leads. The purchasing manager asks questions on SCRM, so her employees also carry out SCRM – and at the same time reduce their costs. That's nothing spectacular. What's spectacular is: How the heck did this risk awareness get into this purchasing manager? Where did it come from?

The most important thing in the world

In complex networks the crisis is not the exception, but the rule.

Risks in global networks are still being massively underestimated at both the strategic and the operational level. Anyone who needs an example only has to open their eyes: We are currently in one of the worst financial crises ever and everyone behaves as if this crisis is an unfortunate exception, a passing disruption. This is reflective of the basic lack of understanding of networks.

There is never a day without at least one mid-sized crisis. That means, frequency alone justifies a massive effort in improving risk competency: Risks in complex networks are mainly identifiable by their disproportionality in damage.

Disproportionality in damage – admittedly, a cumbersome expression. It simply means: small effect, huge cause. A mechanical engineer presented a new switch recently, to a supplier which could replace the old one. The supplier was pretty proud of his innovation. The dimensions and characteristics of the new switch were exactly the same as the old ones. The new one was cheaper, designed in a modern way and more ergonomic. Because there was no obvious change in the specifications, the switch was ordered and installed. Well, actually: almost installed. Because shortly before the old stock was used up, an engineer in production had the typically engineering-like idea, to install the switch as a test to see how it works. Not on its own, of course. There were a few other little changes to be made to the machine.

The switch was installed, the machine turned on, the production parts went through – everything A-OK. At least if the engineer hadn't run the entire machine through an ECG, as it were. And this showed that the new switch, under certain conditions induced a 20 percent higher on-load current. An extra charge that was not planned for, and which for all intents and purposes didn't pose a threat to the machine; however, it activated the machine's safety mechanism, which then automatically shut down the machine, meaning: Every single time that it was turned on. The engineers, who were present at the test, rolled around laughing: »That's the first on/off switch which really does what it says. Whenever you turn on the machine, it turns itself off again!« Imagine what would have happened, had the manufacturer installed the switch five hundred times that month. Could that have happened with a local supplier?

»Not really«, says the test engineer. »Our old switch supplier was from France. He flew in with two other people each time, before making a new offer. He tested even the tiniest new screw in our machines himself. Because every good engineer knows that something looks different in a workshop than on CAD. The new Brazilian supplier could not, of course, afford to do that for such a small switch, the travelling expenses alone would ruin him!« And that is exactly the risk no one had on their minds. Or worse: Someone picked it up on their radar – who wasn't a network pilot. It was just »a damned engineer!« as the CPO of the company spouted that evening over a bottle of red wine: »Why didn't our people discover that? How can we ever carry out ›early involvement‹ when we are showing time and again that we are unable to manage the technical risks of procurement in global networks?«

In the bottleneck of every network, the Single Most Important Factor is the risk.

Just think: A tiny, little switch for 1.50 euro would have cost the company millions in guarantees and lost orders in a competitive market. That is the disproportionality of risk in complex networks. In the bottleneck of every network, the Single Most Important Factor is the risk.

Risk management is not just a method. It's a generic concept of supply chain management: A metaprinciple of network management: If you have risk under control, you have the network under control. Or as a network manager once told a service provider: »You can do everything right for years. And be really good at it. But you'll miss a risk once, and it will wipe away all previous success in one go.« A sad example of disregard for this principle comes from a Western European conglomerate that we'll take a look at.

Jumping without a parachute

Five months ago, suppliers began dying out in the global supply chain of a conglomerate in a way the world had never seen before. The strange thing was, that it was happening equally in all their areas of business. It didn't matter which industry the company purchased in, their suppliers went down like dominos. Most of them ›without any warning‹.

A board member contacted a neighboring SCM Institute, with whom they had worked together on a few research projects in the past: »Do something with our risk managers to get them fit! They have to be able to recognize these failures much earlier and have emergency plans in the waiting!« The company set aside a six-digit sum for consulting and training. The institute could have really used the money, but they turned the work down.

The board member reacted with surprising calmness. Not a touch of anger, indignation or incomprehension. On the contrary. After a conversation with the head of the institute he was the height of contrition. He said under the seal of anonymity: »Actually, we're the ones who really are to blame. We kept the prices down for every one of our suppliers for so long in the past, pressuring them into carrying out every possible investment and research, that we should have been doing ourselves, that in the good years they were not able to build up any reserves. And now, in crisis, they are going down and taking us with them.« You can see similar things going on in the automobile industry, which is why Professor Tom Callarman from the China Europe International Business School reasons: »The question which comes up in light of the crisis in the automobile industry is: What is systematically and fundamentally wrong with the concepts and theory of the American and European automobile industry?« The answer could be given in biblical fashion: You cannot create risks with the right hand and expect the left hand to avoid them.

The head of the institute put it like this: »The company jumped without a parachute and expected its risk managers to somehow put the breaks on the middle of a freefall. He could have saved himself the wasted effort.« By jumping with a parachute.

The training of risk managers alone is not enough: Even the supply chain strategy has to be formulated in a way that avoids risk.

The company now does that. They gave up squeezing their suppliers until it hurt, and have entered into strategic cooperations with some of them in the areas of research, development and investments. The costs are no longer shifted to one side, but shared fairly and above all in a way that reduces risk. Risk is no longer being carried by the suppliers alone, because that had a boomerang effect.

Up until now, the widely used corporate risk strategy was: »Beggar thy neighbour!«, a British saying which means put pressure on your suppliers until they are forced to go begging. That may save money in the short term. However, as the disproportionality in networks shows, it yields only short-term profits: If the supply chain begins to wobble and shake, it will hurt the company applying the pressure to a greater extent than all the short-term cost savings of the past amounted to.

If supply chain risk management is standardized and coordinated, risk protection increases exponentially for everyone.

The conglomerate not only stopped squeezing its suppliers. It actually compells them to carry out risk prevention, ensuring they have some reserves. It even supports them in this effort. This costs more than before, but it creates a synergy effect with improved cooperation. The board says: »We've all been pushed more closely together, we communicate with each other in a way we didn't before.« You could almost say: A lone warrior can do little against a horde of attackers. However, when the supply chain pulls together, building a circle of defence, enemy fire such as risks is easily deflected.

A true synergy effect, which means: It's not enough to train supply managers in risk management. Even the strategies have to be changed so that they don't constantly produce risks themselves. In the company mentioned above, this has happened, but not for most of its competitors on individual markets. Why not? Let's go up in the air for an example of a certain industry.

Aerial combat

Can you extend your hand to a risk? Can you invite it to coffee? No. Because although ›the risk‹ has just eaten up a billion euro, forced millions of people into unemployment and put a crack in the careers of hundreds of thousands of managers (or in other words, has caused very concrete damage) in its very nature it is something totally abstract. It is almost like radioactivity: You can't see it, hear it, smell it, feel it or taste it. You can only see its effects. And these have grown.

Risks belong in the same category as other intangibles like morality, justice, fairness, corporate social responsibility, character, leadership, charm ... Those are primary success factors, which are totally abstract. Until they become virulent, they are all just in your head. That's a dangerous place to be, as a current BrainNet survey ascertained when questioning 204 purchasers in international companies, with an average purchasing volume of 1.2 billion euro, because the risk in the managers' heads is inconsistent.

86 percent of those interviewed said that they put most of their effort into managing supplier risks. That's new. Isn't purchasing meant to be mainly pressured with costs? Or supplying the different departments? Since when is it mainly managing risks? It becomes even more mysterious when 86 percent of those participants totally aware of risk are contrasted with the mere 2 percent who expect to probably or very probably be confronted by supplier breakdown and unpunctual or faulty deliveries at some point. You can draw from this that 98 percent of managers believe their risk management is so good it can avoid, prevent or eliminate all risks. This means the current crisis is most likely just a figment of our collective imagination. Or just one of those marginal ›left over‹ risks, that couldn't be eliminated.

There is a huge gap between your own and someone else's evaluation.

There is also another explanation: Generally, many managers believe that they are very competent in dealing with risks. This optimism is wide spread in management and absolutely justified, if not necessary. Managers and company owners who were not optimistic, would never invest their time and money or found a company. It only becomes dangerous when this optimism crosses over into denial, which happened recently in the aviation industry.

This industrial branch has shown clearly that self-confidence in things like risk management can be exaggerated and that there are glaring differences in competence as with all other abilities. These differences in risk management can determine the life and death of a company, whether they remain intact or are taken over. It can also determine whether staff is reduced or the company expands. That's also new.

Looked at in this way, the recent kerosene crisis acts as a field experiment in risk competence. A kind of grand slam of risk management, as it were. It definitely separated the wheat from the chaff. Like in a laboratory experiment where all the test persons were subjected to the same conditions: The costs of fuel rose up to seemingly unstoppable heights in 2008. All airlines suffered incredibly as a result. The risk of continued increases in kerosene prices was and is palpably near. The task at hand was the same for all risk managers: Protect your airline from the horrendous costs of rising kerosene prices!

The individual risk manager's performance results in this challenge show more clearly than any survey could, how good their individual risk competencies were and above all which glaring differences existed among them. If risk management is really as good as companies think, then every airline should be in the same position. That isn't the case, however, not in the slightest.

The best European risk managers obviously work for Lufthansa, British Airways and Ryanair. The less successful for Air France-KLM, Austrian and Easyjet. Where do the differences arise from?

Panicking and signing last minute contracts are not a benchmark of excellent supply risk management.

By 11th of June 2008, the price of oil increased to a record high of 147 dollars a barrel. Back then even serious analysts were predicting a further increase of up to 200 dollars. That's why »many airlines signed so-called ›hedging contracts‹ sometimes almost in a panic and at astronomically high prices by today's standard,« commented Jens Flottau in German newspaper the *Süddeutsche Zeitung*. Then disaster struck: The oil price first stalled and then decreased by almost 70 percent. Because the airlines couldn't get out of the hedging contracts, they had to pay well over the market price for kerosene. Even if the use of the word »panic« is debatable: It explains a few things.

Fuel prices have been increasing for decades. Why should this suddenly lead to panic actions? Because in the past the kerosene risk had been dealt with in silence. It wasn't managed. And when it suddenly needed to be managed out of corporate political reasons, many companies panicked, because the prerequisites for professional supply risk management were not in place, for example, the ability to carry out simulations.

It's not enough to know only the classical risk tools. Hedging is one of these. But how useful is a hedging expert who can't do simulations? Every hedge is more or less the validation of a scenario which the hedging is based on. If you can't simulate, you can't hedge.

Relying on the evaluation of a ›serious analyst‹ in risk management, is a risk factor in itself, as the German newspaper reported with hardly mistakable malice: How reliable these scenarios from the supposed experts are, was shown by Moody's and Standard & Poor's before the last financial crisis. Anyone wanting to do risk management has to write their own scenarios. Best Practice has recognized this: Our scenario expert, Dr. Heiko von der Gracht, got almost no sleep in the past few months because of a deluge of requests to implement internal company simulations. I look at that with both humor and a touch of sadness. Of course, I'm happy that so many companies in Best Pratice want to learn how to use scenarios. But why did it take a financial crisis for them to get the point?

Some complain that an internal company simulation center costs money. That is a weak argument. A simulation center doesn't cost billions of euro. Yet, that's how much the ›false speculation in hedging‹ cost United Airlines in the final quarter of 2008 alone, according to a Merrill Lynch evaluation. Air France-KLM incurred a loss in the same quarter of around 200 million euro and paid more than twice as much for its fuel. Ryanair's risk managers on the other hand were either totally canny or just asleep: They didn't insure themselves against anything really and are now profiting merrily from the reduction in prices.

In hedging, risk management either uses »swaps« or »put and call« options. The latter allow for more flexibility, but are incomparably more complex than swaps. Only the really good risk managers can use these instruments. That's why Lufthansa is one of the few airlines that works with puts and calls in hedging – and benefits from it during a crisis: Their fuel costs are sinking in the current year by more than a billion euro. These savings can even balance the losses in turnover expected this year, as UBS experts believe.

Good risk management not only protects against risks, it increases profit.

That is a nice surprise! While other airlines complain about the crisis, Lufthansa actually profits from it! The crisis not only offers Lufthansa a new chance, but turns out to be a veritable gold mine for them, because their supply risk managers are the best in the industry. That puts the spotlight on the importance of risk management:

Risk management is more important than the product.

If you think that only applies to the aviation industry, with their extreme dependence on kerosene, think again. It's just this kind of superstition which points to the lacking risk awareness in companies and the media. We all depend on it. This dependence reaches as far as our garbage.

A life in garbage

Until recently anyone going to the outer city limits could witness a strange, new phenomenon: Garbage disposal companies expanded as if the world was going to end tomorrow. They built new sites, halls, and recycling plants. They went massively into sales of secondary raw materials such as wood pellets and scrap metal. At the same time China was grabbing every ounze of metal it could get its hands on, practically ripping out old train tracks from under East German trains to smuggle them into the Orient. Scrap metal prices soared into the stratosphere. The providers of waste disposal logistics earned money by the bucket-load and had their banks finance expansions they'd never dreamed of before. Then crisis hit.

Since then the prices of raw material went down the drain. Some secondary raw materials, such as recovered paper, have lost half their value. Other secondary materials that were once traded like gold are either not in demand or not traded any more. A few companies already face ruin. Because the market crashed? No. Because risk was falsely assessed.

When you think about it, they didn't really assess it at all. They only asked themselves whether they could pay for their loans from their current business earnings. They didn't ask: How will my business be running next year? Will this boom continue forever? How likely is that? These questions weren't asked, because there was an absence of the necessary risk awareness and risk competence, including the obligatory risk manager, who is still missing today. Another thing that comes as no surprise: Many banks don't have them either! Because at the end of the day, they were the ones who gave the waste disposal companies all the loans which are now shaky.

A company's risk is determined by the complexity of its networks.

Aviation, waste disposal, automobile industry, energy business – these industries are not the exception in having an extremely high dependence on and a tendency towards risk. In the meantime every industry faces this risk: A company's risk is no longer determined by external factors such as the scarcity of raw materials, it has much more to do with the complexity of its networks. That means: Risk management is to network management what driver's licences are to driving. Every network manager should have a risk manager as a co-pilot. That assumes, of course, that they listen to their co-pilot. And that's no small feat.

The automobile industry is one of the few industries, for example, in which almost all of the leading manufacturers support their own simulation teams. Didn't they see the crash coming? Actually, they did. There was obviously no one listening in the important positions.

The integration of risk management determines its effectiveness.

In the past companies often did not listen to themselves. Every good controller can tell you a thing or two about it: He knows better most of the time, but no one will listen to him. That is business as usual to a certain extent. How catastrophically this tradition affects risks in global networks, can be seen in the current financial crisis: There is at least one inofficial risk manager in every company, who can assert, quite rightly so, that: »I told you months ago!« Unfortunately, no one listened to him.

In the summer of 2009, the Mexican Flu took its toll on the world. A manufacturer of retail weighing machines has been purchasing and producing in Mexico for 20 years. Because he has network experience, he's had his own risk management group for five years now. This group issued a warning of the risk of an epidemic three years ago: »Hygienic conditions in most households, heat, lacking medical infrastructure … promotes the risk of epidemics!«, said the group manager back then. He passed on these risk assessments promptly to purchasing and the Mexican side as well. What happened? Nothing! Because communication is not management.

Management instead of communication

The crisis shocked many managers. That's why a lot of them send their employees by the dozen to training courses on risk management. That's good. But it's not enough, as the example of the weighing machine manufacturer shows: The ›risk‹ project group saw the Mexican flu coming. They even made suggestions on how to handle a breakout of the epidemic. Instructions which nobody followed.

Riskmanagement must be defined, agreed upon and then trained as a process from beginning to end.

It's not enough to train risk managers. All managers and employees who are dealing with networks and/or procurement have to be trained, starting with the management board all the way down to the Mexican receptionist. The fact that this obviously didn't work for every company in the otherwise paragon automobile industry, doesn't enhance one's confidence in the matter. However, it increases its necessity.

The senior risk manager at the weighing machine manufacturer really believed that it was enough to tell purchasing about the threat of an epidemic. This is naïve even for a rational person. For a risk manager it is downright negligent. A negligence that he is not responsible for: His risk management trainer only taught him various risk tools. The trainer was an instrument trainer. He knew next to nothing about process management. Otherwise he would have told his participants how they could transfer the tools' results throughout the different levels of the company. This defect had to be erased by one of our coaches.

He met with a completely frustrated senior risk manager, who was on the verge of quitting: »What's the use of being able to precisely predict 90 percent of all risks – when no one will listen? I'd rather just quit and try my luck at another company which listens to its experts!« In the first place that would have been a shame, and in the second place, a waste of time: There are hardly *any* companies listening to their own risk experts. Especially, in view of the raging crisis: Even if companies wanted to listen, they don't know how, because they lack the processes for listening.

Riskmanagement means: Every single level in the supply chain knows how to react to a warning of risk.

The supply manager responsible for Mexico went through the roof, when he heard in one of our coach-initiated two person coaching sessions that he obviously hadn't listened to his supply chain risk manager: »What on earth are you talking about? Of course I listen to you! I read your memo! But what was I supposed to do about it? Stop all the deliveries to Mexico? Activate my second source? Pretty quickly I would have gotten an ear full from the purchasing managers!«

When the problem finally reached the board, chaos really began: Two board members pleaded for immediate activation of the second source, as soon as WHO's warning of an epidemic reached level 2. Three board members thought that was totally unnecessary.

As long as risk management is communicated as a suggestion, you might as well forget about it.

Either the company engages a risk consultant for the processes in the company in addition to a risk trainer for the employees or it invests in something that we've been talking about for the previous 200 pages: Develop Leaders! A leader in risk management can achieve necessary process coordination via lower level pathways as well. After three months of risk coaching the senior risk manager of the weighing machines manufacturer had aquired this leadership competence, too.

Because his board was still debating it, he arranged an appointment with his purchasing manager and persuaded him to take the initiative on his own. After that, he coached him to push through this idea in the purchasing department. Since then there is a clear definition of how a purchaser should react when the risk group issues a warning. Corresponding procedures were trained in a half day workshop with the help of some risk simulations. Training was carried out by the senior risk manager. He said: »Why should I wait for the board to make a decision? I can carry out a workshop on my own initiative.« That's how a leader speaks – after going through leadership development. Meanwhile, the Mexicans have also pricked up their ears.

Although they ignored all warnings coming from distant Germany in the past, now they would really like to profit from a fresh breeze in supply chain risk management. Since the board still has not reached a consensus, a coalition of purchasing managers, risk management and Mexican supply chain managers have agreed to devote the next annual get-together of all global locations to this purpose: They plan to spend a half day first discussing and then agreeing upon the standard processes in risk management. This announcement alone provoked a feedback process already.

Since the risk group no longer just issues warnings, but discusses standard reaction processes with their partners in the supply chain, both parties are actually talking to each other. »Suddenly, suppliers and branch managers are calling me from all over America giving us their assessments of current risks,« the senior risk manager says. That looks a lot more like network management to me: The network talks to its management colleagues. By the way, the senior risk manager and the head of purchasing have become good friends in the meantime.

That's because the head of purchasing has realized the imparity of the modern risk situation: »We can save half a million every quarter, just by buying cleverly – and then a new risk comes along and costs a million a week! That's unacceptable. I'm not letting all the months of hard work be ruined by an unacceptable risk in the supply chain in one week!«

Modern risks don't have a gradual effect, they have an extreme effect: They can create extreme damage.

The possible extent of damage was not apparent in the old, national and international networks. That's the reason why one was able to manage them practically as an ›afterthought‹, which is no longer possible. Anyone wanting to manage networks has to be able to manage their risks and to be able to do it in a global context, which means in foreign countries. This can be either totally frustrating, or a lot of fun.

Firefighters in foreign countries

Some risk managers are actually allowed to travel. Recently, one of them went to look at the production plant of a South Vietnamese supplier. He almost got a heart attack: »Are you crazy? Storing chemicals together without a dividing wall?«, he raged throughout the workshop. Even a fifth grader knows from his chemistry class what happens when you mix the wrong chemicals together. What happened after the lecture? Nothing. Four weeks later the local purchasing representative reported that the tanks were still stored directly next to each other without any protection. The risk manager lost it: »If they explode, our production will be completely ruined for weeks! And that is our single source! Should the purchaser build up a second source, only because they can't build a protective wall?« No.

Risk management in global networks requires intercultural competence.

At some point the local purchasing representative had mercy on the risk manager and told him: »You brushed the Vietnamese up the wrong way with your aggressive communication style. They're different from us. They will stop talking to you completely if you don't treat them with respect and politeness.« So he invited the purchasing representative of the Vietnamese production manager to dinner. He asked about his family and listened to his stories about production. He then let it be known that he was really worried that the production manager's great production performance could be endagered by a stupid accident, which would happen if the contents of the different tanks reacted with one another. A week later there was a protective wall: »We can do that, too,« said the risk manager. »Next time it's my turn to invite you to dinner.«

A lot of managers still don't understand the importance of communication skills and intercultural competence. Risk managers always complain to me: »I've been trying my best to be understanding for months with a network partner in … (emerging market). But it doesn't help!« This doesn't mean that trying to be understanding is wrong. It only shows that most global risk managers still have a lot to learn.

There is something like an international escalation scheme.

The typical German usually finishes off negotiations before he starts them: He'll be rough at the start. The typical Englishman has trouble getting away from the beginning: He stays polite even when he should stop. Maybe the two should meet in the middle: Politeness and respect almost always help. If they don't, you need to make your network partner believe in the possibility of a long-term partnership. If that doesn't help, your frustrations need to be communicated moderately, without accusation. If that doesn't help, try agreeing to mutual goals with monetary or other incentives. Only when that doesn't help, should a threat to end the partnership be considered.

Quite a lot of effort, isn't it? That's just one way of looking at it. The other is: Recognize what is there.

The highest maxim in risk management in global networks is: Recognize what is there.

Risk really is complex and explosive in global networks. We should accept it the best we can: So we take a look at what's there – but we don't leave it the way it is. Blatant ignorance of this simple maxim gave us the last global financial crisis: We didn't want to collectively recognize that the global networks are as explosive as they are. If we can accept that and move forward, then this crisis was almost worth it.

At the Edge of the Universe

If you are still with me, hats off! These last pages were really hard work. The leadership gap is putting a lot of pressure on all of us. Particularly in view of the bleak outlook ahead, because we will continue to experience crises in companies, industries and economies as long as we don't have enough real leaders in the responsible positions. We need more leaders.

The current condition of the world and its networks demands this with an urgency that few have recognized up until now, for even if the economy bounces back, the shortage of leaders will stay with us, making us vulnerable to the next crisis. Quite apart from the fact that not being a leader isn't any fun … If you had the choice, what would you rather be?

None of us want to only work and slave. We want to achieve something worthwhile, make a difference, bring a ground-breaking project to fruition, guide the best networks and earn the recognition of our peers and our employees' respect. And we want to have people around us who have set their hearts and minds to these exact, same goals.

Where do these people come from and how should their talents and skills be developed? I hope that the preceeding pages have given you some useful information. If this book helps you on your personal path to leadership, as well as on your way to developing your employees into leadership personalities in global networks, I'm glad. I wish you every imaginable success along the way.

Develop Leaders!

The jury of the International EBS Award

The international jury of academics and management board members put together a shortlist of ten of the best concepts from over 50 competing entries from all industries and many countries. The final winner was selected from this shortlist – after a highly animated and exciting discussion.

Asia

Professor Dr. Dr. h.c. Rolf D. Cremer is Dean and Vice-President of the China Europe International Business School (CEIBS) in Shanghai, China.

He was born in Germany, and received his MSc in Industrial Engineering (1974), and his PhD in Economics (1978) at the Technical University of Darmstadt, Germany.

His experience in China and Asia spans almost 25 years, beginning at Tongji University, Shanghai (1982). In 1983, he joined the University of Macau, where he was Professor of Economics, Dean of Social Sciences, and founding Director of the China Economic Research Centre. In 1992, he joined Massey University, New Zealand, as Head of Economics, and Pro Vice-Chancellor until 2002. From 2000 to 2003, he was the International President at the East China Institute of Technology. He returned full-time to China in January 2003, as Professor of Economics, and – since 2004 – Dean and Vice-President of CEIBS. He is also a Distinguished Professor of Nanchang University, Jiangxi, and Honorary Professor at the Frankfurt School of Finance & Management. In 2008, he received an Honorary Doctorate from the European Business School, Wiesbaden.

As one of the most experienced Deans in the international arena of business schools, he is a member of leading international organizations and boards for shaping the future of management education.

Professor Anil Gupta earned his PhD degree in management from Kurukshetra University (India) in 1986 after his masters in Biochemical Genetics in 1974 from Haryana Agricultural University, Haryana.

He is currently a professor at the Centre for Management in Agriculture. His unique work analyzing indigenous knowledge of farmers, artisans and pastoralists and building bridges to science based knowledge has led to the honor of being elected at a young age to India's National Academy of Agricultural Sciences and recognition through Pew Conservation Scholar Award of USD 150,000 from University of Michigan. In addition, he got the Asian Innovation Award – Gold of FEER, Wall Street Journal, adjudged as one of the fifty most influential people in the field of intellectual property rights around the world in 2003, Padma Shri National Award, one of hghest civilian honour, given by the Hon'ble President of India on the eve of Republic Day January 26th 2004 for distinguished achievements in the field of management education, adjudged as one of the Star Personalities of Asia among the fifty leaders at the forefront of change by Business Week, etc.

His Mission is to demonstrate the potential of knowledge rich economically poor people in taking developing societies out of the morass of mediocrity and lead these on to a path of sustainable progress.

His desire to develop a platform to recognize, respect and reward local innovators was the stimulus behind the creation of the Honey Bee network. The name Honey Bee was chosen to reflect how innovations are collected without making the innovators poorer and how connections are created between innovators. Honey Bee network has demonstrated that by building upon a resource which poor people are rich in, that is their knowledge, a new paradigm of development can be created.

Europe

In April 1991, *Roland Busch* joined Deutsche Lufthansa AG as a management trainee in Corporate Controlling. On completion of the trainee program, he was employed as Assistant Manager in Corporate Controlling from October 1992. In September 1995, Busch was appointed Executive Assistant to the CEO of Lufthansa Group. From May 1996, he played an influential role in the Group's cost-cutting »Program 15«.

In January 1998, Busch was appointed Managing Director of Lido GmbH Lufthansa Aeronautical Services, a company spin-off from the Lufthansa Group. From February 2001, he was in charge of Corporate Audit at Lufthansa. In March 2004, he took over the Group Finance Department, where he was responsible for corporate finance, treasury, financial planning, payment transactions and worldwide fuel management.

In June 2006, Busch joined the Lufthansa Cargo Executive Board. As Executive Board Member, he was responsible for Finance & Human Resources.

Dr. Roland Busch was appointed a member of the Lufthansa German Airlines Board of Lufthansa German Airlines on June 1, 2009. He is responsible for Controlling, Human Resources, Industrial Relations, IT and Purchasing.

Professor Christopher Jahns studied Business at the Phillips University in Marburg, Germany and received his PhD at the Technical University of Munich where he was promoted to Professor.

He has been at the forefront of the European Business School (EBS) since June 2006, first as Rector and then in April 2009 as President. Prof. Jahns is head of the SVI-endowed Chair in Purchasing, Logistics and Supply Chain Management and is Executive Director of the Supply Chain Management Institute (SMI), founded by him in 2004, at the EBS. In addition, he is chairman of the board of the BrainNet Supply Management Group AG and has been a Member of the Board of the BVL, the German logistics association, since 2007.

In February 2009, Christopher Jahns was selected as one of the Young Global Leaders in 2008 from the World Economic Forum.

Randolf Jessl has been the Chief Editor of *personalmagazin* since September 2005. The German magazine, published by the Haufe Media Group, is the market leader in German Human Resources Management.

Mr. Jessl was previously the Deputy Chief Editor of *personalmagazin* and business editor of the German business magazine *Markt und Mittelstand*, published by Axel Springer AG.

Randolf Jessl came to journalism through his studies in Sociology and the Humanities, an internship with Asahi Press, Tokyo, a stint as a volunteer for a daily paper and a vocational training in bookselling and publishing.

Professor Valery S. Katkalo (1964) is the Dean of the Graduate School of Management, St. Petersburg University. He received undergraduate and doctoral degrees in Economics from St. Petersburg University, and did postdoctoral program at Haas School of Business, University of California (Berkeley). He was visiting professor/scholar also at business schools in France, Germany, Finland and Denmark. His research focuses on evolution of strategic management theories, and network organizations. Professor Katkalo is co-founder and co-editor of the *Russian Management Journal*. He is member of the EFMD Board of Trustees, CEMS Strategic Board and of several corporate and University Boards.

Stefan Kurrle is CEO of DHL Supply Chain in the Central Europe Region with around 11,000 employees. Since 2001, he has been heading the Deutsche Post DHL contract logistics business in Germany, Austria and Switzerland. During this time, he has overseen a variety of merger and outsourcing projects that made DHL the industry leader in the region. Prior to this, Mr. Kurrle held various management functions at the BASF corporation.

Sven T. Marlinghaus has been a partner and Managing Director of the BrainNet Supply Management Group AG, one of the leading, international brands in Supply Chain Management Consulting, since 1999. Sven T. Marlinghaus has over 14 years experience in industry and consulting within a wide range of sectors. His expertise includes cost reduction programs, Best Practice procurement process design and the strategic transformation of purchasing departments. He focuses on the automobile, healthcare, software/IT and food sectors.

In addition to his function as a member of the management team, as Chief Communication Officer (CCO), he is also responsible for the global Marketing and PR of the BrainNet Group.

Before joining BrainNet, he worked in the automobile industry for many years, where he was responsible for corporate controlling as well as cost reduction programs in North America, South America, and Spain.

He is the author of many publications in the area of Supply Chain Management, publisher of the BrainNet Science Edition and a regular guest speaker as well as a moderator at trade conferences. He also serves as a jury member for renowned awards such as the Procurement Leaders Award, the Weconomy Award and the SMI Award. Sven T. Marlinghaus has a degree in Business Administration. He is a German national and speaks German, English, French, and Spanish.

Klaus Richter was appointed Executive Vice President Procurement of Airbus effective as of November 2007. He is in charge of all procurement across the entire Airbus organisation, of developing strong partnerships with suppliers and ensuring timely delivery of all purchased goods on-cost and with the proper quality.

Before his appointment at Airbus, Mr. Richter was Senior Vice President Materials Purchasing for BMW, based in Munich, Germany. In this position he was heading supplier relations across the entire company.

Mr. Richter graduated from the Technical University of Munich where he obtained a doctorate in Mechanical Engineering in 1991. After graduation he received a Humboldt scholarship and spent two years as a researcher and teacher at the University of California at Berkeley.

Following his studies, Klaus Richter began his professional career with McKinsey&Company in 1993 as a management consultant. His focus areas were the operational functions in Automotive, Electronics and Aerospace industry. He left McKinsey to join the BMW Group in 2003.

USA

Timothy R. Fiore, C.P.M., Senior Vice President, Supply Management at Terex Corporation is responsible for establishing a company-wide Supply Management and strategic sourcing process. Using a central category management and leadership team, Tim's group leverages the spend across 48 global manufacturing sites of Terex to more effectively manage Terex's $7.3-billion of direct and indirect spend. Terex is a global designer and manufacturer of construction, material handling, mining and material processing equipment.

Tim joined Terex from Celanese Corporation, a Dallas based $6.3-billion hybrid chemical company, where he was Senior Vice President of Supply Management. Previously, he was Senior Vice President, Supply Management, Chief Procurement Officer and President, Ryder Energy Distribution Company, a unit of Ryder System, Inc.

Prior to joining Ryder, Tim was employed for 23 years by United Technologies Corporation companies in a series of procurement and Supply Chain Management capacities. Tim was on the team that led the centralization of that company's procurement activities which resulted in the award of the Medal of Professional Excellence by *Purchasing Magazine*.

Steven A. Melnyk, CPIM, is Professor of Operations and Supply Chain Management at Michigan State University. He is the lead author of 13 books focusing on Operations and the supply chain. He has also authored over 60 refereed articles. He is a member of the editorial boards of three Supply Chain Management related journals.

Prof. Melnyk is also the Director of Education for the Purchasing Management Association of Canada. His current research interests include Supply Chain Management, Supply Chain Design, Supply Redesign, Process Management and Control, Metrics/System Measurement, Transformation Management, and Environmentally Responsible Manufacturing (ERM).

Prof. Melnyk is an active researcher whose articles have appeared in numerous international and national journals. Currently, Prof. Melnyk, in conjunction with faculty from several American, European, and Canadian universities, is working on the SCM 2010 and Beyond Research Project.

Andrew K. Reese is Editor of *Supply & Demand Chain Executive,* which is published by Cygnus Business Media of Ft. Atkinson, Wis. Reese joined the magazine in May 2000, and he is responsible for development and oversight of editorial content and production for the magazine. Reese has more than 15 years experience in research and writing.

His prior experience includes time as a consultant for a public relations agency in Moscow, Russia, dealing with accounts for leading Western technology and consumer-products companies entering the post-Soviet market. Previously, he worked as a writer and editor at Washington, D.C.-based nonprofit organizations. In addition to *Supply & Demand Chain Executive,* Reese's articles have appeared in *Purchasing Today* (now *Inside Supply Management*), the *Journal of Supply Management, Fabricating Equipment News, Plant Safety & Maintenance, Private Air, Tycoon* and elsewhere. His translations of Russian articles have appeared in the *Nation magazine,* the Law in Eastern Europe series

(Institute of East European Law and Russian Studies), *Russian Conservation News* and elsewhere. Reese holds a BA in Journalism from Arizona State University and an MA in Soviet Studies from Harvard University. He resides in the Phoenix area.

Acknowledgements

First of all, this book could never have been written if some of the world's best companies had not given me access, in the most generous way, to the secrets of their success. My thanks go to all Best Practice members, those whose names are mentioned and, in particular, to all those who shall remain anonymous. I would also like to thank Christian Rast and Thorsten Schiefer for their active support on this and many other projects, along with all my colleagues at BrainNet. My special thanks are given to the President of the European Business School (EBS), Prof. Christopher Jahns. He was an enthusiastic driving force from the beginning of this project about learning from ›the Best‹. Thanks also to my team at SMI Executive Education at the Supply Chain Management Institute who supported me not only with the manuscript but, above all, with the considerable preparations for the »Develop Leaders!« Award. And last but by no means least I want to say thank you to my partner, his family, and my parents who lent me their emotional and moral support, particularly during the long nights in the manuscript phase.

Nicole Gaiziunas
September 2009

Index

W

About the author

Nicole Gaiziunas has turned her fascination for the olympic ideal into a career. She advises, trains and coaches the Best in a discipline that affects our modern life like no other – global network management. Born in the German city of Bad Hersfeld, in Hesse (famous for its theater festival every year) she went on to do a degree in Business and Social Studies, joining a team at an international management consultancy directly afterwards.

She plays golf with a passion in her limited freetime and sees it as a metaphor for management development: »Golfing is like top management -- talent requires training.« Today she is the Managing Director of the SMI Executive Education division of the European Business School. She provides consultancy services, with 80 academics and in cooperation with 220 consultants, to international board members and top executives, training and developing highly qualified network managers, currently one of our rarest business resources. Although she advises and coaches the »rich and powerful«, in private she's got both feet on the ground, enjoying time at the weekend with friends and family. She writes as she talks, coaches and advises – openly, directly, and with a friendly wink of the eye.